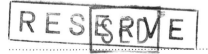

Cricket for Schoolboys

The author

Cricket for Schoolboys

Phil Sharpe

(Yorkshire C.C.C. and England)

PELHAM BOOKS

First published by
PELHAM BOOKS LTD
26 *Bloomsbury Street*
London, W.C.1
1965

© *1965 by Phil Sharpe*

Set and printed in Great Britain by Tonbridge Printers Ltd,
Peach Hall Works, Tonbridge, Kent, in Times eleven on
thirteen point, on paper made by Henry Bruce at Currie,
Midlothian, and bound by James Burn at Esher, Surrey

CONTENTS

ILLUSTRATIONS

CHAPTER ONE

APPROACH TO THE GAME

Attitudes towards cricket are changing with a rapidity almost out of keeping with our most stately sport. The West Indians have seen to that. In fact, 1963 was one of the most momentous years in the long history of cricket. When I left Worksop College in 1955, as captain of the first XI, I would never have imagined that less than ten years hence amateurs would have disappeared almost completely from the first-class game, a knock-out competition amongst the counties would have completely captured the imagination of a now very choosy sporting public, and Test match grounds would have echoed for day after day with loud sounds of praise, ribaldry, delight and disgust. Thank goodness for the innovations of 1963, and most of all for the West Indians!

Our visitors from the Caribbean had already injected life into an apparently dying game in their triumphant tour of Australia. They did an even better job – if that is possible – in England in 1963.

County cricket had been slowly but steadily losing its spectator appeal – although it was never a great crowd-puller. While millions still follow the progress of the county of their birth, residence or fancy, they choose to do so mainly through the mediums of radio, television and newspapers, all of which have never failed to satisfy their appetites. One has only to walk around a ground on which a county match is in progress to realise that the majority of spectators nowadays are retired, elderly people, with little else to do to pass away the time in the twilight of their lives than take a packet of sandwiches, a Thermos and a travelling rug to the county ground for the day – day after day. There is still the usual quota of autograph-hunting schoolboys, but their attentions, as television cameras have shown us, are devoted mainly to games of cricket amongst themselves.

There are exceptional games, of course, which still draw the crowds in their thousands – the Roses battles are still almost as popular as ever – but nothing has been more pathetic in recent years than a visit to Old Trafford when any other county but Yorkshire have been playing there. Such a fine ground so nearly empty goes a long way towards explaining the slump in Lancashire's fortunes of late. (I hope things will improve in future years.) How can a team be expected to play entertaining cricket in such funereal surroundings?

Generally speaking, the young have turned their backs on county cricket in an age when more and more people are participating in sport and leisure activities rather than remain in the passive rôle of spectator. More money, the motor car, boredom with their jobs – all these have been factors in a revolution that has had far more drastic effect on other sports than cricket.

County cricket – the three-day variety – is dying because it too often fails to entertain. And the players are not wholly to blame for this. Covered wickets, indifferent weather, and lack of incentives have played their parts, too. Is it fair to expect a man who is playing for a place in his county side, and whose livelihood, and that of his family depends on just this, to parade his full array of strokes with carefree abandon? I don't think so.

This, of course, is the basic difference between county and schoolboy cricket. One is a game – the other too often a job of work, and no more. Much of the enjoyment of cricket has evaporated – for the professional performer.

Dull as it often is, there is still, however, much to be learned by the schoolboy from county cricket. When at school, cricket is too often played because it is compulsory to play the game. Some masters and coaches regard an afternoon's cricket as a bit of fun, or a rather pleasant way of passing the time. Some of them are really totally ill-fitted to coach boys in the arts and techniques of a very complicated game. Some of them have had very little experience of serious cricket, and judging by the way they allow their charges to place their fields, it would seem that they have been unwilling to spare the time to learn even the fundamentals of the game.

It is generally recognised that Yorkshiremen take their cricket far more seriously than most, and this is particularly true at county level. If the Yorkshire county side is not always winning, plenty of people want to know why. Winning is almost all-important in Yorkshire, and in this aim we are far nearer to the aims of some other nations in their attitude to sport than are the natives of some of the southern counties of England.

Players like Brian Bolus, a Yorkshire colleague of mine – until he joined Nottinghamshire – have told me about the enormous difference in attitudes they have experienced. Playing for Nottinghamshire, Bolus has been able to go out to play his strokes from the start of an innings, with no one to reproach him for making a 'duck', and plenty of praise for his hundreds. Consequently he has made a big impression on the scene, and become an opening batsman for England. Obviously, the lifting of the mental burden from his mind of *having* to succeed has made Bolus a far better cricketer. That he has become just this has been very evident in the carefree way he has made such a lot of runs in recent seasons.

But this relaxation of the tension would not suit everybody. There are plenty of men who rise to the occasion when success is demanded of them, and would become very ordinary players if this tight mental discipline were to be relaxed.

I would never advise every schoolboy to play their cricket the Yorkshire way – in fact I find it difficult to do so myself. I try to treat each day, with its success and failures, very much as it comes. But I have absolutely no time at all for the masters whose attitude makes it plain that the game's the thing, and never mind the technicalities.

This is all very well for those not particularly suited to or attracted by cricket, whose only intention while playing it *is* to while away another afternoon before moving on to more stimulating pastimes. For the boy who is adept at and keen on the game, this lackadaisical attitude to its technique is disastrous. He acquires none of the tactics and strategies that are so important a part of the game, while his softened attitude will make him singularly ill-fitted to the demands of senior cricket.

I say that boys should decide early as to their attitude to cricket. If they are to take it seriously, there can be an exciting and pleasant life for them in first-class cricket, and, if they are outstandingly talented, glittering financial rewards. And although there is much in county cricket to be ignored and disregarded, there is also much to be learned. How much better it would be for our cricketing future if county cricketers were able to spare the time to visit schools to coach during their careers, rather than at the end of them, when their enthusiasm may have been blunted by the six-days-a-week grind, and certainly their mobility will have decreased. If schoolmasters are to be allowed to coach their boys, let them at least take the trouble to strike up a nodding acquaintance with the intricacies of a fascinating game.

For the boy who has no intention of taking the game seriously, and who has no great aptitude for it, I would proffer the advice to play as well as possible without making it an imposition. There is much enjoyment to be had in cricket at lower than county level, and, as a schoolboy, it is surely less tedious to try to do a thing reasonably competently, rather than adopt that awful 'couldn't care less' approach?

Who knows? You may be better at the game than you think.

How then, should one start to play cricket? One of the game's drawbacks – in the eyes of many – is its changing laws, which would be difficult enough to master were they to remain constant. You should hear Freddie Trueman on this subject! Master the laws of cricket, and their application, and abide by them. The old chestnut 'it just isn't cricket' may be a sneer at the game, but it illustrates the point that cricket and cricketers will not tolerate 'rule benders'. If you are given out, don't stand about gesticulating that you could not have been l.b.w. because your left leg was in such and such a position. If you know that you've snicked the ball to the wicket-keeper or into the slips, don't wait for the umpire's finger to be raised after the appeal. You know if you're out, and if you are, well get out! Nothing looks worse than the batsman who is given out, but stays behind to argue. And do not appeal for catches that are not catches – the ones you scoop off the turf so often in the slips. Do not appeal for catches when you know the batsman's wave at the ball has been nowhere near to making contact. Remember that the umpire is standing more than twenty-two yards away – and all umpires are fallible. Learn the laws thoroughly, stick by them, and you will enjoy your cricket all the more.

Watch the great cricketers as often as you can, and I mean study them. If you find it difficult to concentrate for long periods, try making your own scorebook. See how the great batsmen use their feet to make stroke-play look easy. See how their timing of the shot makes it look effortless. Anyone who saw Ray Lindwall will know just how effortless a perfect bowling action can make the job appear – and Freddie Trueman is not far behind in this direction. This fluency either at the crease or in the field can only be achieved by one thing – fitness.

Just because it is played at what many people today regard as a snail's pace – such is the rush and hustle of modern life – do not presume that you can play cricket when only half fit. Hours in the field will soon convince you that this is very far from the truth. Remember that you may be called upon to bowl for far longer periods than you perhaps bargained for, if your opponents get on top. How dreadful it would be if you had to say: 'Sorry skipper, I just can't manage another over.'

Just as surely, matches can be won by really quick, intelligent running between the wickets, and certainly nothing looks worse than batsmen who dawdle over their first run, and, if they get the chance, get progressively slower over the next two.

Only by being one hundred per cent fit is it possible to be on top of your job. Cricket makes tremendous demands of your concentration. A long innings is not possible without it. Catches are dropped by the dozen by fielders whose concentration has crumbled at the vital moment.

Remember that cricket is a team game. You owe it to your team-mates to be fit enough to cope with any situation that might arise – which means very fit indeed.

CHAPTER TWO

THE ART OF BATTING

Everyone loves to see a fine batsman flaying the opposition. This is the greatest delight in cricket. The batsman is far more often the hero than the poor journeyman bowler. It is high scoring, not great feats of bowling skill and endurance, that the crowds really turn out to watch. The majesty of Ted Dexter in full cry, the fluent ease with which Colin Cowdrey strokes the ball with dazzling speed to every boundary, or the sheer brutality of the famous hitters like Harold Gimblett, and nowadays, Yorkshire's own eagerly anticipated Freddie Trueman, are the crowd-pullers. So let us turn our attention first to batting – the art of batting.

As in golf, the grip is of tremendous importance, for the right-hander the left hand being positioned above the right on the bat handle, and vice versa for the rarer left-handed batsman. The hands must be kept close enough together to be able to work together. If they are placed too far apart, the tendency is for them to work against each other, with the consequent loss of timing and touch. Some batsmen prefer to hold the bat low on the handle, but they are rare, and, ideally, it should be gripped as near to the top as possible to allow full control of the blade.

So position the left hand first, with the back of the hand facing the bowler, and the left elbow raised to face him too. The right hand supplies most of the power to your strokes, and is positioned so that the back of the hand faces your stumps. This hand does the pushing, and should be square behind the handle. The left hand, as in golf, is responsible for controlling the stroke, and should never be allowed to slip behind the handle.

The bat handle must be gripped firmly but not too tightly. A tight grip ruins the timing, and just as obviously, too loose a grip will allow the bat to be pushed rudely aside by the weight of the ball. Now try swinging the bat with a pendulum motion, never allowing the left elbow to flop in towards the body. This will cause the bat to be twisted towards the body, with the resulting hooking or smothering of every shot.

Before going any further, it is necessary to explain that as one faces up to the bowler the stance is also of paramount importance. The normal orthodox stance is achieved by placing the feet not too far apart – never wider than the width of your shoulders. Keep the weight forward on the balls of the feet, so that you are instantly ready to move in any direction. Never allow the weight to be transferred to the heels, or you will be caught immobile and off balance should the ball spin in or away from you. The left eye has a full view of the bowler as he moves in and bowls, and of the ball in flight. Some batsmen favour a two-eyed stance, with the head and body turned further towards the bowler, but this presents a bigger target to the bowler, in that the right leg is visible. One is thus more susceptible to

B

the ball that leaves one – the out-swinger. More about that later.

Back-lift is also really a matter of preference, but those batsmen who play with hardly any back-lift of the bat are seldom the attractive stroke-makers – too often the plodders who are doing so much damage to the game – but are so difficult to get out. Obviously by lifting the bat high as one shapes to make a stroke, one offers the bowler a view of the stumps – his target – and – and gives the ball a chance to get through.

The answer is to lift the bat as far back as you feel necessary to apply the maximum power to the attacking stroke, and the necessary power for the defensive stroke. The back-lift must inevitably be far greater for the attacking strokes, and need be negligible if one is merely intent on smothering the spin as one stretches forward.

The basic movements of the feet to make strokes are fairly simple. The left foot moves forward for the drive or a defensive forward stroke, the right foot back and slightly across the stumps when one plays a defensive shot, or an attacking one, to the ball that pitches short.

The bowler's one aim is to pitch the ball on that elusive spot on the pitch which is just beyond the batsman's forward reach to turn the ball into a full-pitch or half-volley, and too close to him to enable him to play back with certainty or safety. This is called the good length ball, and prompts such phrases as 'So-and-so quickly found his length . . .' in reports of cricket matches.

When I was a boy being coached, I used to take the

bat back in an arc away from my body towards the slips, and was told that this was all wrong, and that I must try and take the bat back straight. I am not sure that this matters as long as the bat comes down straight, although if you take it back straight there must obviously be more chance of it coming down straight. I make this point in passing on to our next phase, because although I have laid down a general rule above, I do not think cricketers should be bound by too many hard and fast rules. There have been many famous cricketers who had their idiosyncrasies of style. No one asked them to change their style when they were making hundreds of runs. My own conclusion on back-lift is that too much is a bad thing – I take the bat no higher than the stumps.

For those new to the game: the off-side of the field, and the off-stump faces him as he stands up to face the bowler. The on- or leg-side is behind him. The field is divided for this purpose into two halves, a line being drawn between the two sets of stumps and continued to each boundary behind them. The off-stump is furthest of the three away from the batsman. So an off-drive is hit on the off-side, that is in front of the right-handed batsman, and the off-break spins in towards him from that direction. The leg-break comes, as it were, breaking in from behind the batsman's legs, if he were to stand still. The away- or out-swinger is a ball that swings across the batsman's body from leg to off, and an in-swinger swings in to his body from the off.

I pause to explain this because a lot of cricketers nowadays will tell you to watch where the seam lies in the bowler's hand, as he comes up to bowl. Seam bowlers, as those who swing the ball or use the seam on the ball to move it either way off the pitch are called, particularly stress this point. In this way they claim the batsman can see which way the ball is going to swing, according to the bowler's grip. I do not think it is particularly wise to follow this advice. You talk to some bowlers and they will tell you that they hold the seam upright, and even they do not know which way the ball is going to swing. And if the bowler does not know which way he is going to swing the ball, the batsman has little chance by watching his hand.

Mind you, as far as spin bowling is concerned, I regard it essential to watch the bowler and his hand like a hawk. You must be able to tell which way the bowler is spinning the ball.

It is easy to tell an off-spinner by the way he tweaks the ball at you. You see the tips of his fingers as he spins the ball. But the leg-spinner, with his flick of the wrist as he rolls the ball out of his hand, is much similar to the googly merchant's action, and there are many batsmen playing in first-class cricket today-who cannot distinguish between the two actions, although there is a basic difference that is quite obvious when explained.

The leg-break bowler rolls out the ball with his fingers and palm from the underneath of the hand – his hand is on top of the ball as it is released. The googly, being the leg-spinner's off-break, comes from the back of the hand.

Gary Sobers told me that he was able to pick up the ball and know where it was going to land the moment it left the bowler's hand. Obviously if you can do this, you can move your feet quicker, and be in position ready to play your shot with plenty of time to spare. But this represents the difference between a great player and a good player, and if you are able to pick the ball as it leaves the hand, as does Sobers, you are in the great class! Of course the difference between being in form and out of it is demonstrated in much the same way. When you are in form you will find that you are picking up the ball more easily, and putting your feet in the right position. But when you are in poor form, and not getting many runs, you will struggle, and find you will not pick up the ball so well, and your footwork will be all over the place.

The essential thing to remember, therefore, is to try to pick the length of the ball as soon as possible, and once you have done that, your feet adjust themselves accordingly.

In county cricket there is a technique which will be strange to most schoolboys, unless they have watched much first-class cricket – the bat and pad technique. This is only employed on a turning wicket, or a wicket that is favourable to spin bowlers. If the ball is turning a great distance, the left leg is thrust as far as possible down the wicket with the bat behind it, so that if the ball is going to turn a lot it is going to hit the pad, and not the bat, and you are not going to be caught by any of the short legs. There are some cricketers who play bat and pad all the time, and they are terribly dull to watch. These are batsmen who are helping to kill first-class cricket. Bat and pad should be reserved for bad wickets.

On good wickets the batsman must be playing with the bat all the time, and using his feet to get to the pitch of the ball. County cricket is also cursed by batsmen who are fast-footed, and will not venture forth from the crease to play their shots. It is against this type of batsman that the spin bowler has a field day. He has the upper hand from the start if the batsman has not the courage to try to drive him off his length. The technique of bat and pad is valuable, however, for the first two or three overs on a turning wicket, until you start picking the length of the ball properly.

The basic difference between county and schoolboy cricket is in the wickets, which makes the transition from one to the other a difficult thing to accomplish without hardship and a struggle. At school, I found that I played mostly on very good wickets and as a result I tended to become a little lazy in technique. The ball is always coming through straight, never deviating, and the tendency is to play with a stiff right hand, not relaxed as it should be. Away from school, wickets are not so good, probably a little softer, and the ball does not come through as truly. Consequently you have to adjust your technique to combat the change of pace off the pitch. You find, for instance, that the ball turns more easily off a soft wicket, and it will move off the seam, and if you start playing this type of ball with a stiff right hand, or stiff jab as they say, you will probably be cocking up catches right, left and centre.

Sometimes I think if I had gone straight from school to play in another county, and on better wickets than are found in Yorkshire, I think I should have got further in the game than I have. When you play on good wickets at school, good wickets at University or in the South of England, your technique develops from your surroundings, and Test matches are always played – or almost always – on good wickets. I have mentioned this to several of my colleagues in the Yorkshire side, and they reply that if this had been the case, I would not have had my experience of turning wickets. But how many Test wickets turn?

CHAPTER THREE

THE STROKES

When I first came from school into Army cricket before playing for Yorkshire Colts, I was told by Maurice Leyland (in the nets at the start of the season) that I would have to get out of the habit of playing square-on, which is so dangerous when playing back. I think that as a young boy I did this because I was constantly being told that I must always be behind the ball, and I found myself getting too far behind it thinking about it, and getting into the square-on position. Fortunately I have now managed to cure myself of this habit. It is just a matter of practice at the nets – the best place to get rid of any bad habits. It is a bad habit to get square-on, because you are particularly susceptible to any ball leaving you, especially the out-swinger. The two-eyed stance does on occasion give you an advantage against the in-swing bowler, however. If the ball is coming down the leg-side often enough, if you are square-on you can lift it over the field – over mid-wicket.

I am of the opinion, as I said in the previous chapter, that it does not really matter where you take the bat back as long as it comes down straight, although it is obvious that you are more likely to achieve this if you do in fact take the bat up straight. I have also decided that it is not too good a thing to lift the bat up too high on taking it back – just take it as high as the stumps.

The drive is probably as fine a shot to watch as any, when timed well, and one of its finest exponents in the game today is undoubtedly Ted Dexter. He is such a good player that he is able to play the ball, as we say 'on the up'. That is to say, the ball is not necessarily a half-volley, but Dexter just puts his foot down the wicket and hits the ball as it comes up off the pitch, using his customary high back-lift and following straight through just as fully.

But the half-volley is by far the easiest ball to drive, and the good players appear only to lean on the ball to make it speed to the boundary – the impression given by good timing. If the ball is pitched on the leg-stump or just outside it, the on-drive is employed, the ball passing anywhere in the area around mid-on, and as far round as mid-wicket.

To drive, the left foot must be thrust down the wicket as near as possible to the pitch of the ball – bat and pad as close as possible at all times. Naturally enough it is the straight ball that is usually driven straight, and just as naturally the ball that pitches on the line of the off-stump or outside it that is off-driven.

The cover-drive is employed to the ball that pitches still further outside the off-stump – about six inches outside it – further if you dare. Again, the half-volley is the easiest ball to cover-drive, and I never saw a better exponent of this beautiful stroke than York-shire's own Sir Len Hutton. With this stroke the bat has to be brought down in something of an arc when the left foot has been put right across and as near to the pitch of the ball as possible once again, and the ball is driven anywhere through an arc of about 45 degrees between extra cover and cover point.

As I have said, I favour a back-lift that does not take the bat above stump height. Peter May was one of the best batsmen I have seen who favoured the same short back-lift, but conversely there are few finer cricketers in the world today than Sobers, who has one of the longest back-lifts in the game. But, as I have explained, Sobers is able to afford the luxury of this full swing because he sees the ball so early.

The square cut is seen less and less in county cricket because of the defensive mentality that has entered the game. Nowadays it is considered the height of stupidity to be caught behind the wicket or in the slips, cutting at a short ball wide of the stumps. Yet this type of ball is the easiest to cut square to the boundary, and this should be its fate. Bowling in county cricket has improved so much that the opportunities to play this shot are limited by the non-arrival of many bad balls. It is, however, nonsensical to say that attacking shots cannot be played to good balls. They are, however, much easier to play when there are seventy or eighty runs to your name on the scoreboard, and this is particularly true of the square cut. This stroke should really be played off the back foot, although Ken Grieves has scored hundreds of runs during his career with a sort of square slash that is played off the front foot. The shot should be played by putting the back foot right across in line with the ball, or as near as one can get to it, and the bat brought down well on top of the ball, as it is struck square to the wicket, as the name of the stroke implies. The danger of the shot is that if the ball is snicked, the wicket-keeper is usually provided with the easiest of catches off the edge of the bat. These mis-hits usually occur when the feet are not moved, and the bat is 'hung out', or waved at the ball as it passes.

The great Herbert Sutcliffe always used to say that one should never cut until September, which gives some idea of how dangerous this shot can be, but is not so dangerous or difficult to perform as the late cut. Sir Len Hutton played this shot to perfection.

Here again the ball has to be short enough to play late, and the right foot is placed back and across, and the ball played downwards in the direction of third man. It is a good shot to play when a slow left-arm bowler is turning the ball away towards the slips, and he has six men in the covers, but not often a short third man. Whenever the covers are packed, and you are struggling to get the ball through the field, the late cut is a valuable shot. It will usually mean that the short third man will have to move finer to cover the shot, which causes the men in the covers to move round, and give more room to play the cover-drive, and get the ball through.

Ranjitsinghi was reputedly the finest player of the leg glance in cricket history, but I was not on the scene to witness his brilliance. What I do know is that 'Ranji' played the ball at catchable height, a yard or two off the ground. Nowadays he would never get away with such a shot, which is what most people fail to realise when

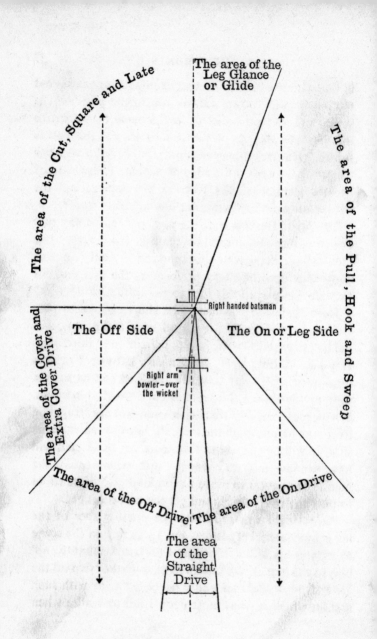

criticising county players for leaving alone balls that are passing down the leg side. With the development of in-swing bowling has come the placing of two men behind the wicket on the leg side, which heightens the risk of being caught out 'round the corner'. There is not so much leg glancing in modern first-class cricket because players will not attempt the stroke unless they are certain they can keep the ball down. Cyril Washbrook was a tremendous player of the stroke – so skilled in keeping the ball on the turf.

The shot is played in a similar manner to the on-drive, except that the face of the bat is turned at the last moment to an angle that allows the ball to slide off it obliquely, instead of being met with the full face of the blade.

The hook and pull shots demand a quick eye, lightning reflexes, and considerable courage. They are both back foot shots which can only be played off the short ball, and more often than not bring about the batsman's downfall if he tries to hook or pull a ball of fuller length. This almost always causes the ball to strike the bat far too high up, thus allowing no force to go behind the stroke. More often than not, the ball will lob gently to a leg-side fielder in these circumstances. If you asked me to differentiate between the hook and the pull, I would say that anything that passed behind the square-leg umpire was a hook, and anything that passed in front of him was a pull. We had a tremendous argument about this with the Australians on a Cavaliers' tour of South Africa. Some of them put forward a theory that anything that stayed on the turf was a pull, and anything that went in the air was a hook. It does not really matter.

What does matter is that you must keep your eye on the ball all through the stroke, or you have no chance. Of course, this is true of every shot, but more true of these attacking shots than any. The back foot must be taken back and across, and the head kept inside the line of flight of the ball, otherwise one is asking to be pinned between the eyes! The ball is swept away with all the power at the batsman's command, with the bat at the horizontal. Sobers has the wonderful knack, and has such powerful wrists to hook and pull anything remotely short of a length. He whips the ball over mid-wicket without apparent effort, but for less great batsmen, this is essentially the most violent shot in cricket.

The sweep has never been one of my best shots, and I have always regarded it as rather dangerous to risk. Generally it is employed against the off-spinner, because in placing the foot well down the wicket, and across outside the line of the stumps, it is not possible to be trapped leg before wicket, if the batsman fails to make contact.

The sweep, as the name implies, is played with a horizontal movement of the bat to propel the ball to leg, but in its execution, the batsman's right knee is on the ground as he reaches to play the ball at ground level, on the full- or on or about the half-volley. It is more difficult to sweep against the spin served up by the leg-spinner, but is also hazardous against the off-spinner capable of bowling the top-spinner that hurries straight on without turning in on the batsman. A straight top-spinner pitched in line with the stumps that deceives the batsman when he is down on one knee must trap the batsman leg before wicket, and with the present leg-before-wicket rule in operation, this is one of the few ways one can be trapped and given out when on the front foot.

My Yorkshire colleagues, Brian Close and Doug Padgett, are fine players of this sweep shot, and use it particularly on turning wickets when the off-spinner is pitching way outside the off-stump, and they cannot be trapped leg before wicket. Close is marvellously adept at going forward, realising the possibilities of the ball during its flight, and altering his shot at the last moment to a controlled sweep.

As for lifting the ball over the fielders' heads, I think this inadvisable unless you find yourself bogged down by accurate spin bowling. When this situation arises, it is always a good thing if you can lift the ball over the field, particularly over the bowler's head. If you manage to do this once or twice, the bowler will have to move a man back in anticipation of further attempts in that direction. This will widen the gaps in his field, and you will perhaps be able to take your singles and twos, when previously you were unable to score. Only when chasing runs against the clock would I advise lofting the ball over the close field, unless you are a low order batsman incapable of playing the more academic shots!

Running between the wickets is one of the most important and most often neglected facets of batsman-ship. There are so many occasions when runs are missed, singles especially. And when the ball appears to be going towards the boundary, and looks as though it is certain to go for four, it is infuriating to watch batsmen caught in two minds, cantering their first run. When the ball is stopped inches short of the boundary they sometimes find that they have thrown away at least one run, probably two. It is absolutely essential to run the first run as fast as possible, whatever the circumstances, once the mind has been made up to run, and this must be done very quickly and decisively, if there is to be no misunderstanding, and the probability of a run-out. If the first run is taken fast enough, there is usually time for one or two runs more. Unless you know that the fielder to whom the ball has gone is a magnificent athlete, and has a tremendous arm, it is almost always safe to take a run for the throw. If my memory of schooldays serves me right, we used to miss hundreds of runs by failing to follow these elementary rules. So learn all about your fielders – whether they are left- or right-handed. If a right-handed fielder is stationed at cover point, and you push the ball to his left, you can rely on a quick single without much danger, and so on.

It is up to the batsman to learn how fast the opposition is in any position. There are runs all round the field, there for the taking, if only one is looking for them. This can be seen at a county match, when one side is going for quick runs, and the game becomes virtually tip and run. The ball has only to be stopped by bat, and even pad, for the batsman to be scampering down the wicket. Runs as short as these depend very largely on the batsman at the bowler's end, who must

Ted Dexter shows all his power in straight driving

The dangers of the sweep. Dexter bowled round his legs by Bobby Simpson, the
Australian captain, one of the best leg break bowlers in the world

be backing up to stand a chance of making his ground. Matches are lost and won by running between the wickets fast or otherwise, and more so than ever before now that the Gillette knockout Cup competition between the counties allows each side only 60 overs at the wicket.

There is also a tremendous art in calling for runs. The general rule about whose job it is to call is common sense, in that the batsman taking strike must call if he hits the ball anywhere in front of the wicket or square to it, because he is better able to see where the ball is going when it passes the batsman who is stationed at the bowler's end, and who should be following up anyway. Conversely, the batsman at the bowler's end must call when the batsman taking strike hits the ball anywhere behind his stumps, because the striker can then only see the path of the ball by looking behind him. This he has certainly no time to do. If there is any doubt as to the safety of a run, the batsman whose call it is should call 'wait', and then 'come one' if he decides a single is on. Just as surely, he must call 'come two' if he is certain that two runs are available, because this will encourage his partner to take the first run as fast as possible. Even in county cricket, when team-mates are playing alongside each other six days a week, there are many, many misunderstandings over calling for runs which cause run-outs.

There is no more unsatisfactory way of getting out in cricket, and when a man runs one of his team-mates out, perhaps more than once, the whole spirit of the team can be undermined. To run out a partner can only

give rise to resentment. For this reason it is essential to
avoid what we call the 'deaf and dumb show', which
can be seen far too often in county cricket. On these
occasions neither batsman calls, with the result that they
too often progress down the pitch in a series of irri-
tating fits and starts that can be suicidal. Although
matches can be lost and won on the running between
the wickets, there are no prizes for taking runs that
don't exist, and it is better to say a decisive 'no' than
embark on a run that isn't there. I am trying to bang
the point home that calling must be loud and decisive,
and the decision to run or stay at home must be taken
as quickly as possible – which is, as I have already said
– no more than common sense.

On arrival at the wicket to begin an innings, the first
step to be taken is to take guard. This is done by
holding the bat as upright as possible in a position that
you think is as near as possible to covering the stumps
from view by the umpire standing behind the stumps
at the bowler's end. There are three commonly accepted
forms of guard used in modern cricket, and of the three,
leg stump is the most common. That is to say that
you wish the umpire to tell you when your bat blade
covers the middle and leg stumps, and when he has
guided you to this position, by a series of hand signals,
it is up to you to make a mark on the pitch so that you
can take up this position at will from then on.

The other guards are centre, which as the name implies, means that the bat covers the middle stump, but
part of the off- and leg-stumps are exposed, and leg-
stump. This latter guard is asked for more often when

the ball is turning, and the batsman is anxious to avoid a leg-before-wicket dismissal by keeping his legs as far from the target as possible, but really all three guards are chosen as a matter of preference.

Never feel embarrassed about asking for guard several times in an innings, if the mark you have made on the pitch has been obscured, and you are not sure where you are standing in relation to your stumps. These are the bowler's target, and if you leave your stumps exposed in error, do not blame the bowler for knocking them down. It is not his duty to tell you that you are not properly defending your wicket, nor is it the duty of the umpire – unless he is asked. It is common practice among county batsmen to take a fresh guard after completing a hundred runs, or even fifty, as this gives them the sensation of starting all over again, with the consequent feeling of freshness that helps to fortify their concentration. But it is more common to see a batsman take a fresh guard to greet the arrival of a new bowler – again a matter of no more than common sense. If a bowler changes from bowling over the wicket – that is, with the stumps on his right as he delivers – and *vice versa* for a left-hander, to round the wicket, it is a good idea for the batsman to take a new guard. This is because more often than not an off-spin bowler will change from bowling over to round the wicket when he finds that he is able to turn the ball a considerable amount, and is therefore going for a leg-before-wicket decision against the batsman.

CHAPTER FOUR

THE ART OF FIELDING

Of all the cricketing clichés, none rings truer than the old adage that 'catches win matches'. The side that holds its catches must beat a side that does not, and fielding is tremendously important, in that scores of runs can be saved by efficiency in the field. If there are not too many runs between two sides, and runs are hard to get, and therefore of double value, good fielding can decide the result. It is impossible to have too much fielding practice. In my last year at Worksop, we tried to get in fielding practice of some kind on four or preferably five days every week. We were all keen on keeping our fielding up to scratch, and it is important to realise that if you have a bad day with the ball and the bat, you can still do a very good job for your side by fielding keenly and well.

There are a lot of ways of making fielding practice more interesting. Every school taking cricket seriously – and that should mean every school – should have a slip cradle. We were never off the thing at Worksop. For those who have not seen one let me explain that the cradle takes the form of wooden slats, an inch or two apart, curved to form a cradle-shaped bowl which closely resembles those dinghies with blunt stern and

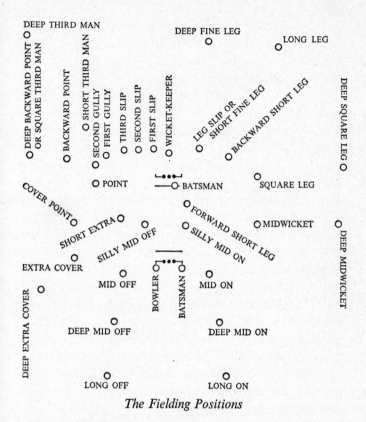

The Fielding Positions

bows. This structure rests on metal feet to stabilise it.
Two or more people stand at each end and throw the
ball hard into the cradle, which sends it flying up and
on in any one of a hundred directions, according to
how it strikes the slats.

This is a marvellously efficient means of practising
slip catches, which are the most frequent type of catch

found in cricket, and are most frequently dropped. Hundreds of centuries have been scored by batsmen who have been dropped in the early stages of their innings, usually in the slips.

Perhaps an even better way of practising slip catches is for a batsman to stand at an imaginary wicket, with two or more slips standing behind him in their appropriate places, and for someone to throw the ball to him fairly hard at shoulder height so that he can slash the ball off the edge. In this way, difficult as it can be unless the thrower throws accurately, and the batsman can find the edge of his bat constantly, real slip catches can be more accurately imitated. The ball can come at the slips at any height, at any speed, off the edge of the bat.

The classic way of getting fielding practice is for one man to stand encircled by the rest of the team. The man in the middle holds two balls, which he whips out in any direction, one at a time. In this way everyone is kept awake, and their reflexes are sharpened. Obviously a fair amount of common sense must be used with this method of practice. For example, the ball must never be thrown to a man if he is looking in another direction for another ball. The West Indians practise with four men standing in a line opposite another line of four, and they throw one ball to each other in a variety of ways, high lobs, hard straight catches, and so on, but always keeping the thing moving.

Another good idea is to give your man in the centre of a circle of team-mates a bat, and toss the ball to him so that he can hit it in any direction. In this way you learn how fast, or otherwise, the ball can come to you off the blade – a useful thing to improve your judgment of this important factor in making catches. The long, high catches that come to the men who field in the deep can best be imitated by a man who throws the ball up, and hits it hard and high to a line of fielders. The easiest way of avoiding confusion and accidents, which can happen on the field when the match is on in earnest, is for the batsman to call out the name of the fielder who should catch the ball.

On the field, there is nothing more stupid to be seen than two fielders, both with their eyes on the ball that has been skied high, colliding when trying to get underneath the ball to make the catch. It is the job of their captain to call out the name of the man who is in the best position to make the catch, whenever possible, but if he does not do so, then one of the two or more men going for the catch must shout 'it's mine'. This is a difficult decision to make, and becomes very embarrassing, temporarily, if you should drop the catch, but it is far preferable to a painful and unpleasant accident that could put one or more fielder out of the game – injured.

There is a great technique of slip catching. I have made something of a speciality of the job, and seldom field anywhere else, and it is no secret that I was supposedly selected to play Test cricket for England against the West Indies in 1963 when I was batting badly, but there was some need for a specialist slip fielder, since many catches had been going down there. This is a fine example of how important slip fielding is regarded by the Selectors.

It is my opinion that when you are standing at first or second slip you should watch the ball. If you are wider, at third or fourth slip or in the gully, then you should watch the bowler. I always watch the ball from the moment the bowler starts his run up to the wicket, and follow its line when he releases it.

The difference between a great slip fielder and just a good one is in the quickness of the eye and reactions, and judgment of the speed of the ball. In fact, I would put this last point first in importance. And you must never stop trying to quicken up your reflexes.

I always get down into a position in the slips so that my elbows could be resting on my knees, except that I never allow them to do so, in case they hinder movement to take a catch. The distance away from the wicket at which you station yourself can usually be taken from the wicket-keeper. I always take my spot – when playing for Yorkshire – from Jimmy Binks, who judges what he thinks will be the pace of the ball from the wicket, and stands in a position to take it easily. If he finds that the ball is not coming through as fast as he thought, and is dropping at his ankles, he moves up a yard, and so do the slip fielders. Likewise, if the ball is flying, then you all move back a pace. Jimmy Binks does not like his first slip to field too close to him, but the usual distance as first slip takes up his position alongside the wicket-keeper is for the men to be about four feet apart. There should be four or five feet between the slip fielders. The best way of measuring the appropriate distance is for the slip fielders to hold out their arms, and touch fingers, and then move about six inches apart, to allow themselves room in which to move.

The Australians like to stand a lot further apart in the slips. They like to have much more room than we do because they like to dive about. On their wickets they get more bounce and lift, and snicks go higher and wider than they do in England. I had an amusing experience when out in South Africa on the Cavaliers' tour a year or two back. I could not get accustomed to fielding so wide at slip and could not get it right at all. I never knew who should dive for the ball when it came between first and second, and could imagine all kinds of painful consequences if both men decided to go for the ball. Richie Benaud was at first slip at the time, Ted Dexter at second, and me at third. I said to Ted that we were standing too wide apart, but he was told by Benaud when he inquired that we were absolutely right where we were. The second ball that came down went between Richie and the wicket-keeper, and I felt like saying 'I told you so', but we all had a good laugh about it. After that Benaud went out of the slips, and I said to Dexter – 'Let's get some sanity back into the game,' and we stood finer.

As I understand it, the Australians believe that a lot of edged strokes go through where a third slip would stand, and if they have only two slips, these fellows have to cover as much ground as possible. But in my opinion it is far better to have two slip fielders standing far closer to each other, where it is ninety per cent certain that they will make the catch, rather than two men so far apart that they are only seventy per cent certain of taking it. Naturally, there is more chance of taking a slip catch if it comes straight at you than there is of grabbing the ball if you have to dive.

Different people have their own peculiar ways of holding their hands when fielding at slip. I hold mine as I would if I was holding a football.

In any other position than the slips, and the other close in-fielding positions – such as short leg, gully, or short extra – it is absolutely essential to remember to walk in as the bowler runs up to deliver the ball. A useful tip is to keep moving even when the ball has been bowled, because it is far easier to get off the mark quickly in any direction if you are already moving, and don't get caught on your heels, which does happen if you stop when the bowler has delivered the ball.

Brian Bolus used to ask me when fielding at cover point or mid-wicket how he could get off his heels. He was walking in with the bowler, and then stopping, and being caught out. You have to think that every ball throughout the innings is coming to you, and you are not going to let any man have a single when you are fielding. This is the only kind of attitude that will keep you moving in, and when the ball does come to you, you will never be caught flat-footed.

Catching in the deep is all a matter of judgment. When you see the ball coming, and you get that funny feeling in the pit of the stomach that it is coming to you, wait a few moments unless you realise that it is going to be a mad dash if you are to have any chance of reaching the ball at all. By waiting for even a split second you will have that much better chance of picking the ball up, and making really sure whereabouts it is going to land. So many bad judges of catches in the deep hare off too soon, and find themselves having to double back, or suddenly change direction in their chase, with the result that their balance is lost, and more often than not the catch is put down.

I once saw Willie Watson, now an England selector, make a magnificent catch in the deep field at Bradford. He waited, saw he would have to run between twenty-five and thirty yards, set off at top speed, paused to sight the ball again, and then set off, to catch it on the run.

By setting off immediately, people fail altogether to allow for the effect of the wind upon the ball. The higher it goes, the more likely it is to be affected by the winds that so often swirl around cricket grounds, just as they do round all types of stadiums, where the grandstands act like huge windshields, forcing the wind to go round instead of through them.

The golden rule about fielding is to get your body between the ball and the boundary, and if necessary – such as on a bumpy ground – get down on one knee to block the ball with some part of your body, should it fly up. This is painful, but essential, particularly on grounds like Bramall Lane, Sheffield, where the Sheffield United football pitch adjoins the cricket arena, and half the outfield is consequently very bumpy indeed.

Another absolutely essential rule, whether fielding the ball, or making a catch, is to get two hands to it whenever possible. There are no prizes for spectacular one-handed catches when two hands could have done the job, and it stands to reason that to catch the ball with one hand is just twice as difficult as to catch it with two. The same applies with fielding, although there can be no objection to a fielder stopping the ball with an outstretched foot if he can get to it no other way, and by doing so he prevents the batsman from scoring a boundary.

Catching is made considerably easier, as for that matter is fielding a ball that is struck very hard, by cupping the hands to receive it, and drawing them back as the ball lands in them. This ensures that the hands are moving in the same direction as the ball at the moment of impact, which takes some of the force behind the shot away, and saves your hands from being badly stung.

Throwing is an essential part of fielding, because it is little use making a fine stop, if you cannot complete the movement with a quick and accurate throw, in the hope of catching the batsman napping and running him out. If there is a chance of a run-out, there is little point in throwing the ball yards wide of the man at the stumps, whether it be the wicket-keeper or the bowler, or another fielder.

To learn to throw accurately to the wicket-keeper is another important part of fielding practice. The throw should ideally be full pitch into the hands of the wicket-keeper or fielder at bail height, but if it is to be a long throw, no one will grumble if the ball bounces once, and then comes to the wicket-keeper at bail height. No fielder or wicket-keeper likes to take the ball on the half-volley, however, or worse still, after it has bounced several times and is only rolling along the ground. Nor is there much chance of a run-out if the ball is hurled high above the wicket-keeper's head – an obvious statement – but this happens very often even in first-class cricket.

Just as obviously the best throw is the quickest to reach the wicket, so if you are fielding close enough to manage it, throw the ball hard and low into the wicket-keeper's gloves, so that the arc described by the ball's flight is a narrow one. A high throw is only necessary from the boundary when the thrower may not be too strong in the arm.

If there is no chance of a run-out, however, or if the batsmen are not even running, there is little point in hurling the ball in at tremendous speed. Much less energy is used up by the fielder and catcher, if the ball is lobbed gently in, perhaps with an under-arm throw. This is another matter for common sense to decide.

Most of the great wicket-keepers are remarkable for their lack of exhibition and complete unobtrusiveness. Instead of showing-off, and making everything simple appear difficult, they accomplish absolutely the reverse, by means of superb anticipation – and of course this is also true of fielding. The effect on the morale of the whole team of a great wicket-keeper has to be seen to be believed. Godfrey Evans was a case in point. Evans had such boundless energy on the field that his busy way of going about his work had a great effect on his team-mates, and kept them on their toes, even when the sun was burning out of a cloudless sky, and they had to suffer the whole long day in the field. If a wicket-keeper is confident and competent in all he does, the fielders will gain confidence from him. Jimmy Binks does a similarly fine job in this capacity for Yorkshire – always cheerful – and always dashing about to keep in the game.

The good wicket-keepers always keep their fielders on their toes by keeping them in the game, too. This can best be done by immediately tossing the ball to one or other of the slips on taking it. Then the ball is transferred either via the leg-side or the off-side field back to the bowler, so that everyone is getting a feel of it, and staying alert. The value of this tactic cannot be over-emphasised for keeping the fielding side on its toes.

As I have said earlier, it is up to the wicket-keeper to take up his stance behind the stumps according to how the ball is bouncing, and carrying to him, when the fast bowlers are operating. If it is possible to stand up to the medium-pace bowlers, then the wicket-keeper should do so. But he will win no praise by standing close to the stumps, if he is continually missing the ball, with the result that the slip fielders are having to chase after it.

What the wicket-keeper must avoid at all costs is standing in no-man's-land, that area where the ball is not quite reaching him at a reasonable height, or is even pitching short of him. Either stand up, or stand right back, but never in between. If you are standing back, remember it is your first duty to get up to the stumps at the first available opportunity to receive the ball from a fielder, so that there is little chance of the batting side being able to grab overthrows.

The matter of stance for the wicket-keeper differs according to taste, but most men crouch down, with their fingers outstretched to be resting gently on the ground, their hands together. You will never see a good wicket-keeper taking the ball with his fingers upwards, unless the ball is flying high over his head. Once again the ball is taken with the hands moving backwards away from it at the moment of impact. Just because the wicket-keeper is wearing gloves, there is no reason to assume that his hands cannot be stung through them, which is why I emphasised the commonsense point that the ball should only be thrown as hard as possible to him when there is a chance of a run-out.

Stumpings are a rare event nowadays in county cricket, but catches at the wicket are still plentiful to those wicket-keepers whose anticipation allows them to move either to leg, or away towards the slips, as he sees the batsman shape to play his shot. The great thing to remember, and this applies once again to fielders, is not to snatch at the ball, but allow it to come to you, and make sure you are ready to hold on to it. To snatch at the ball with heavy gloves on your hands is almost always fatal. Neither must the ball be snatched at when the wicket-keeper is trying to pull off a stumping. This is a difficult fault to avoid, especially when the wicket-keeper has noticed that the batsman raises his right foot by no more than a fraction of an inch now and again. Another point to remember here is that the wicket-keeper is not allowed to take the ball to make a stumping until it has passed the stumps.

To stump or run-out a batsman, there is absolutely no need at all for the wicket to be smashed with a mighty sweep. It is quite sufficient to remove one bail with the hand that is holding the ball. But it must be remembered that the bail must be removed in this way – not with the free hand, with the ball held aloft in appeal in the other.

If the ball is played away from the near-to-the-wicket fielders, and the wicket-keeper makes the decision to chase it himself if the batsmen are going for a run, it is most advisable for him to remove his thick outer glove, so that he can take a shy at the stumps with more accuracy with his thin inner glove on, which does not represent such a hindrance to a quick throw.

Backing up, as it is called, is the hall-mark of a good, wide-awake fielding side. It is done by any fielder who is in the position at the time, or near it, to stand behind the wicket-keeper, bowler or fielder at the stumps, who is about to receive the throw from the outfield. Should the ball be thrown in inaccurately, he is then in a position to gather it if it avoids the man who is the intended target, and no overthrows are given away. It is particularly important to back up the man at the wicket when the thrower is plainly going to attempt to throw down the stumps to run-out the batsman.

There are obvious dangers in being a wicket-keeper. Despite the gloves, the hands are still vulnerable, and when one is standing up to the stumps, and the ball is turning and lifting, it is sometimes impossible for the wicket-keeper always to catch the ball. Sometimes they are caught in the face. But these hazards are nothing

The sweep – as demonstrated by one of its most effective exponents – Brian Close, captain of Yorkshire

Right foot well across, head as near as possible to the line of the ball, Ken Grieves, the Lancashire captain, shows how the cut should be played

Alan Davidson, one of the game's best all-rounders, prepares to deliver a fast ball for Australia. Note the right shoulder pointing towards the batsman, and the impression of power

The late cut. A difficult shot played to perfection by Sir Len Hutton

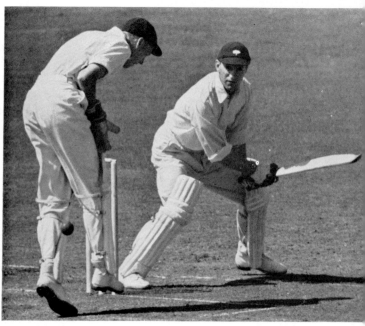

compared with the risks voluntarily taken by professional cricketers in first-class cricket.

Brian Close, the Yorkshire captain, is one of the most daring, or foolhardy – depending on which way you look upon it – fielders in the game. Brian likes to stand so close to the batsman at forward short leg or short square leg that he is almost breathing down his neck, and can be touched by the swing of the bat. By doing this, he puts pressure on the batsman, who naturally becomes afraid of cocking up a simple catch off any ball on or around his legs. Close's close proximity must unsettle him, and never allow him to relax. Other counties are making this position quite a common one, having seen that Close has taken many fine catches there.

But the M.C.C. are anxious to dissuade any schoolboy from fielding in these potentially suicidal positions, and I heartily endorse their view. It is all very well for grown men to take the risk of serious injury. They have a reasonable chance of survival, because the bowlers in first-class cricket, since they are operating six days a week, are more likely to bowl accurately all the time. Schoolboys are extremely unlikely to avoid dropping the odd ball short, and I must remark in passing that one of Yorkshire's most promising batsmen, John Hampshire, was fielding in a similar position early in the 1964 season when one of our lads dropped one short, and although usually the fielders around the leg-side dive to earth as quickly as possible, John was not quite quick enough. He was hit just above an eye, had to have five stitches in the wound, and the usual injection. He suffered a reaction to the injection, and along with the eye injury, this caused him to spend several weeks away from his living. When he came back, he took several more weeks to regain his confidence and form.

No schoolboy can afford to suffer a similar fate, and I must try to impress on you most forcibly that it is absolutely essential that you should take no unnecessary risks while playing cricket. A cricket ball is one of the hardest used in ball games, and although my plea is for schoolboys to take their cricket seriously, to field too close to the wicket is doing the reverse – it is just plain stupidity. It takes months of practice, and sharpening up of the reflexes, to be able to take the kind of catches Close sometimes snaps up. So leave that kind of gamble to him.

CHAPTER FIVE

THE ART OF BOWLING

Bowling is the facet of the game I am least qualified to talk about, because I am always on the receiving end. But it was not always so. At Worksop I wanted to be a fast bowler – what schoolboy doesn't? – but I was far too small for the job.

Fast bowling is the game for the strong and broad shouldered. There are few small fast bowlers, and just as certainly there are very few giant fast bowlers. If you are very tall, the body suffers terribly in the act of bowling fast, and since stamina is one of the prime requirements of the job, tall thin men seldom last as fast bowlers.

There can be no finer build for the job than Freddie Trueman's, although even he could probably do with a little more height. In his hey-day, however, he could bump the ball down as hard as anyone from his medium height. He had the strength to do it.

The taller the man, the more he will be able to pull the ball down hard on to the pitch, and make it rear up off a good length. David Larter, who stands six feet five inches tall, can do this as well as anyone in the game today, but he suffers from being too tall, and has been sorely troubled by injury. So far, Larter, who plays for

Northamptonshire, has failed to make his mark in Test cricket, and I feel it may be because his build is not quite right for the rigours of five-day cricket. Similarly Fred Rumsey, the Somerset star, has the reputation of being suspect in the stamina line, although he stands well over six feet, and is broadly built.

I was a fast bowler at the age of twelve, but apart from being too small I came to the conclusion that this is a mug's game. The perfect thing to be is an all-rounder. If you can bat and bowl with equal facility you always get two bites at the cherry, and if you fail at either batting or bowling, you have always the chance to redeem yourself with one or the other.

All very tiring, but most satisfactory. All-rounders are an invaluable asset to any side. They are the men who are hardest to drop. They seldom get out of form at batting and bowling at the same time. Trevor Bailey is probably the finest example of the all-rounder in present-day English cricket. He seems to have been turning in wonderful performances for Essex for as long as I can remember following first-class cricket.

There are several very important things to remember if you want to become a successful bowler. So many schoolboys who want to bowl fast, for instance, always bowl *too* fast, or try to bowl faster than they really can, consequently losing control of length and direction. And schoolboys are not the only culprits. This thing can happen in county cricket. Many men have made a great success by switching to bowling fast medium, or even medium, gaining much in accuracy to counter-act what they have voluntarily sacrificed in speed.

Remember that even such great fast bowlers as True-man, with 300 Test wickets behind him, can make the mistake of trying to get just a little extra pace to achieve a break-through, and finish up losing accuracy and length, and being hit to every corner of the field. Many people thought this was the reason why Fred lost his place for a time during the 1964 series against Australia. When he came back for the final Test at the Oval, he had decided to bowl every spell after his first off his short run, and was no less effective for that, as his figures showed. So, if you want to be a good fast bowler, settle for a speed you are capable of sustaining for a reasonable period without having to tell your captain that you've had enough –not that there is any crime in that – or sacrificing length and accuracy.

Many cricketers, if they are honest enough to admit it, are more than a little afraid of a good, accurate fast bowler, but few are bothered about the fast bowler who is all over the place, because there is nothing easier to face. You can play your strokes against a fast bowler who is chiefly off the target, and know that only a touch will send the ball skimming to the boundary.

Bowling is much more than just running up to bowl. Half the business is to 'think' the batsman out. To play on his weak spots, and avoid his strong points is essential. Conversely, if you find that a batsman has been at the wicket for some time, and is becoming particularly fond of any one stroke, there is always a chance that he may try to play it to a ball that is not suitable. So there is another problem for you – to try to get him to do just that.

It has always been a favourite tactic against the great Australian batsman, Norman O'Neill, to try to get him to indulge in his favourite hook shot early in an innings, when perhaps he is neither seeing the ball too well, nor timing the strokes. O'Neill would be the first to admit that he has been a sucker for the hookable ball early in his innings, and more so to the ball that is not easily hookable. O'Neill is such a refreshing character by modern standards that he will have a go at anything, and the crowd is usually just as sorry as he is if he gets out, such is his entertainment value. In schoolboy cricket particularly, no one is going to grumble at you for getting out by trying to play your shots – I hope – but in first-class cricket one has to be prepared to be blamed for anything– for playing shots and getting out – or not playing shots and staying in.

There is only one way to becoming a good bowler, and that is to bowl, bowl, and bowl. There are no short cuts. You must always use your head, and always bowl to your field. There is little point in bowling down the leg side when you have three slips and a gully, but how often have you seen it done?

So let us deal first with fast bowling, and seam bowling, which is becoming more and more popular – in the absence of really fast bowlers. The seam, which runs round the ball, is obviously of prime importance to the quick bowler. According to its position in the hand, the ball will swing in either direction. Movement in the air is also helped by the constant polishing of the ball on one side of the seam. The other half of the ball is allowed to wear as quickly as possible. This means

that one half of the ball offers the maximum resistance
to the air it passes through, and the shiny side the mini-
mum resistance.

To bowl an out-swinger, which, as its name applies,
swings away from the right-handed batsman towards
the slips, the shiny side of the ball is on the outside, as
the right-handed bowler makes his delivery. Thus the
brake is put on the inside half of the ball as it leaves
the bowler's hand, which forces it to move from right
to left, or leg-side to off, looking from the bowler's
viewpoint. The seam is usually held upright, and held
in the fingers rather than the hand. Then it should
make first contact with the turf, if the ball swings away
as intended. This fact is most important, as the ball
will tend to turn back fractionally from the off if the
ball does pitch on the seam. This is called a 'nip-backer',
a most dangerous ball if the bowler can make the ball
run away late towards the slips, and then bring the odd
ball back in towards the batsman. To bowl an out-
swinger, the arm must follow through across the body
to help the motion, just as in bowling an in-swinger the
right arm follows through straight down the side of the
body, or even moves exaggeratedly away from the body.
The chest must never be presented to the batsman. The
bowler must always be side on to his target as he delivers the ball.

I cannot over-emphasise the importance of setting the
correct type of field for the type of ball you are bowling.
Field setting is so often a closed book to schoolboy
cricketers, and more often than not to their masters,
who take charge of the day-to-day games, that I shall

indicate on diagrams suggested field placings that should be ideal for the different types of ball likely to be most popular in schoolboy cricket.

For fast or fast-medium bowlers, bowling predominantly out-swingers, there must be two slips and a gully, a third man and fine-leg or long-leg – all behind the wicket. I would recommend a short square leg (but not too short, as I have stressed earlier), a cover point, mid-off and mid-on. If you are bowling this variety of

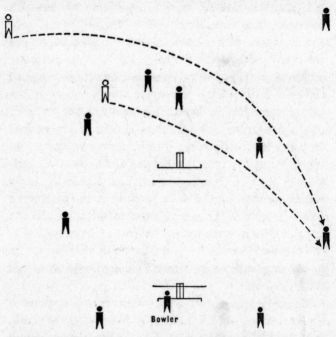

Field for fast-medium bowler bowling predominantly out-swingers. If he is erratic, slip or third man is moved to mid-wicket

delivery, and cannot find your length and direction with any consistency – and provided your captain allows you to continue bowling – it is as well to move one of your slip fielders, or even third man, to the mid-wicket position. This will be necessary if you insist on bowling down the leg side, which is the thing any bowler should avoid. You must bowl in the line of the middle- or off-stumps, and be moving the ball away, to be presenting any problems to the batsman with out-swingers, unless you are swinging the ball a lot, in which case your line should be leg stump.

The ball on the middle stump of good length that moves just sufficiently to take the off is a very good ball, and if you are moving the ball a lot it can be pitched, or aimed on the line of the leg stump. The ball pitched around the region of the off stump, running away, is the one that is most likely to earn you your slip catches, and it is this latter that I would advise any out-swing bowler to concentrate upon. But this type of delivery should never be aimed too wide on the off-side, for the simple reason that the batsman will be able to leave it alone. Too many balls like this and you will soon be banished to the outfield – exhausted!

The object of every type of bowling must always be to keep the batsman in action. By allowing him to leave the ball alone, you are granting him the opportunity to sum up exactly what you are doing with the ball in the air and off the pitch, an opportunity he will gratefully accept – particularly if it occurs early in his innings, when he perhaps is not seeing the ball too well. The ball that allows the batsman to take a breather later in his innings is just as helpful to him. But this type of inaccurate delivery must be avoided at any time. It is the sure way of contributing to negative cricket.

Just as most out-swing bowlers deliver the ball from a position fairly close to the stumps, in-swing bowlers tend to veer away from the stumps prior to delivery – that is if they are bowling over the wicket. This movement is helpful to their action of cutting the ball in towards the batsman, and heightens the impression of diagonal flight across the batsman's body towards the leg-side of the wicket.

Neil Hawke, the big Australian who had such a successful first season in Test cricket against us in 1964, is a man who very often demonstrates this movement. The ball is held as one would expect for this type of delivery, with the seam to the left of the first finger, in a diagonal position to allow it to touch the ground first. Just as the 'nip-backer' from the out-swinger is a dangerous delivery, so the similar thing achieved by an in-swing bowler is a very valuable asset. The right arm at the moment of delivery must be held high for the in-swing to be most effective, just as it may come over lower to help out-swing by the very fact that it is more a slinging type of action this way. The body is more upright for the out-swinger, while it is bent over backwards, if anything, by the in-swing bowler.

The field for the in-swing bowler is predominantly a leg-side one, because three men behind the wicket on that side are allowed in schoolboy cricket, but not in the county variety. Instead of two slips, the in-swing bowler needs only one, and a third man – no gully. A

cover point and mid-off complete the off-side field. A
long leg or fine leg, backward short leg, short square
leg, mid-wicket and mid-on pack the leg-side, where the
ball will almost always finish, as a result of the swing.
Perhaps the most devastating ball in cricket is the in-
swinging yorker, as bowled with such incredible
regularity and effect by the big West Indian policeman,
Charlie Griffith. The yorker is the ball of very full

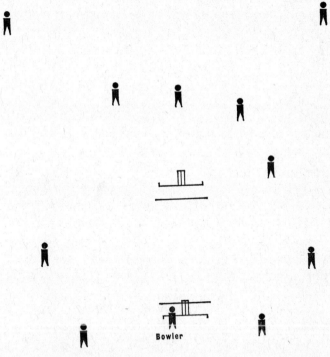

*Field for fast-medium bowler bowling predominantly in-
swingers*

length that passes underneath the bat as the batsman plays forward – almost, but not quite a half-volley – a delivery that has to be dug out and rammed down upon with the bat to prevent it getting through.

A fast or fast-medium left-arm bowler, bowling over the wicket, takes as his target the line of the off stump or thereabouts. He bowls to a field that consists of two slips, gully, third man, cover point, mid-off, mid-on, square leg and long or fine leg. A left-arm bowler coming round the wicket – or to the left of the stumps

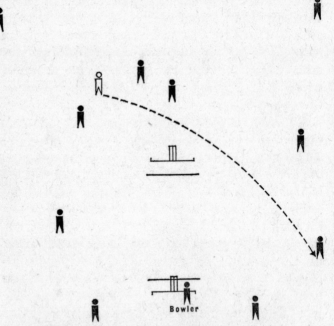

Field for fast-medium left-arm bowler. If he is being pushed through mid-wicket, slip is moved to mid-wicket

– is doing much the same as a right-arm bowler bowling in-swingers. Alan Davidson, the Australian, was the great exponent of this type of delivery, to a packed leg-side field. He would bowl over and round the wicket, according to wicket and weather, and the needs of his side, at a pace from fast down to medium. If the left-arm merchant is bowling over the wicket, and he finds he is being pushed through mid-wicket, then he must move his second slip across to block the stroke.

While we are dealing with the business of fast bowling, there is the vexed question of bumpers. These are hardly within the province of schoolboys, but they are a fairly common occurrence in county cricket, and must therefore be considered, because so many promising schoolboys are being plunged into first-class cricket at an early age – even if it is only in the Minor Counties' competition.

A bumper, or bouncer being a ball that is pitched excessively short, in the hope that it will fly high to discomfort the batsman, is a genuine tactic as a surprise delivery. Used occasionally, on a suitable wicket, it has in this element of surprise considerable value in unsettling a batsman, disturbing his concentration and rhythm – he will always afterwards be wondering when the next one is coming along – or even bringing about his dismissal. The batsman is quite likely to raise his gloves and bat to ward off the ball as it comes at his head, and if he makes contact, even with only a glancing blow, he is quite likely to give someone near the wicket a simple catch.

Excessive use of the bumper, which can only be an

intimidatory tactic to frighten the batsman into an error, a false stroke, or to actually injure him, is *inexcusable*. But there are some bowlers who use the bumper to do just this, despite the umpires, whose duty it is to prevent excessive use of this dangerous ball, and who are supposed to warn off any bowler who they think might be guilty of this despicable ploy.

Bumpers are often used as revenge, when a fast bowler has been harshly treated, and as such are far less dangerous; in that in first-class cricket, one gets to know the type of bowler likely to hit back at one in this way. Generally speaking, the only use for bumpers must be as a surprise tactic, which means that they must only be used occasionally. Far more effective, when bowled cleverly, and hidden well, is the fast bowler's slower ball. Hawke got many wickets (quite a few in the Test matches) with this very well-disguised delivery. But all fast bowlers should vary their pace all the time. A one-paced fast bowler is a poor bowler. Trueman has always been a great one for varying his pace, and swinging the ball both ways.

The actions of fast bowlers are very individual affairs, and some of them seen regularly in this country are quite appalling.

Schoolboys should concentrate in perfecting a good action at an early age, because only then will they be able to realise their full potential. Most of the men who have poor actions get poor results, and their styles were usually formed in schoolboy cricket, because of lack of adequate coaching and supervision.

Trueman's action would be hard to fault, a model of

smooth acceleration and effortless power. John Price, who opened the England bowling with him in 1964, is a fast-medium bowler with a most incredible run-up, starting in the region of a deep mid-off, and progressing to the wicket in a great, sweeping arc. Watching him, one always fears that he will come off the rails.

Generally speaking again, the run-up should be almost straight, perhaps more so if one is bowling mainly in-swingers. Never take a longer run than is absolutely necessary to build up your speed so that you are in a position to put everything into your delivery. Too many fast bowlers make the mistake of starting their run-up at a gallop, and get slower as they approach the wicket. This is quite illogical. If you are a right-handed bowler, the left hand and arm is used for balance, and is moved about accordingly, but raised just before the moment of delivery as the body sways back to get the maximum thrust behind the ball.

Trueman and Lindwall – whose action was probably the smoothest of all – both approached the wicket with their left shoulder leading, and it is essential to turn the left shoulder towards the batsman before delivery to be able to follow through with the full power of the right shoulder, arm and body. So many fast bowlers deliver the ball facing the batsman, which means that their arm only is doing the work. This is an unsatisfactory state of affairs that will almost certainly mean that such a bowler will tire quickly, and be unable to bowl fast for a sustained period.

So much controversy has centred round the actions of fast bowlers in recent years, it is as well to remember that the delivery arm should be kept as high as possible at the moment of delivery, and the arm as straight as possible, unless you want to be branded as a 'chucker'. This was the terrible fate of Ian Meckiff (Australia) and Geoff Griffin (South Africa), who were hounded out of first-class cricket because they either broke the wrist, and flicked it at the moment of delivery, or delivered the ball with a bent arm.

Slow bowlers too can be accused of throwing the ball, as Tony Lock found to his cost on a number of occasions in recent years, to name just one victim of his own misfortune.

Much trouble and controversy has also been caused by the follow through of the fast bowler churning up the pitch with his studs as he does so. Matches have been lost and won by bowlers who have been able to pitch in these patches, which makes their deliveries almost impossible to play. These rough patches are the bane of left-handed batsman especially, who are particularly exposed to spin bowling that pitches in the rough.

Richie Benaud caught England in such a manner at Old Trafford on his last visit to England as captain and leg-spin bowler – allowing the Australians to win a Test match they had appeared certain to lose. England could not grumble, since it was mainly their own fast bowlers who had churned up the pitch.

So remember to follow through sharply away from the line between the stumps. This should be natural, anyway. The in-swing bowler is usually veering towards the edge of the crease, and the out-swing bowler is

Wes Hall, the West Indian generally held to be the world's fastest bowler, demonstrates how he gets his body and full weight behind each delivery

Wes Hall's partner, Charlie Griffith, shows the extraordinary balance required by a world class fast bowler

The ball is about to leave Ray Lindwall's hand. Note the position of the shoulders, and the arched back

bringing his arm down and across his body, which should encourage a follow through away from the stumps.

One of the many recent changes of law – these changes are the curse of modern cricket – is the much-hated front foot rule. For years the bowler had to make sure his foot – the back foot, that is – was behind a line level with the stumps when he delivered the ball. If he came beyond that line, he was automatically guilty of bowling a no-ball, and the umpire had ample time to 'call' him – to shout 'no-ball', which meant that the batsman was secure in the knowledge that he could only be dismissed by a run-out. Suddenly the rule was changed – for first-class cricket only – so that the front foot, which in the case of the right-handed bowler is the left, had to stay between that line level with the stumps and the popping crease, as the next line up the pitch is called. Because the ball is delivered as this foot lands on the ground with some force, it has become almost impossible for an umpire to 'call' the bowler in time for the batsman to have a swing at the no-ball. Bowlers have had to revise completely their approach to the wicket – some have been utterly unable to do so – and because this rule applies only to first-class cricket, one rule exists for a small number of cricketers compared to the large number who are still playing to the old rule. This is the difficult situation that will face any older boy hoping to make a start in the county side – a ludicrous one.

This problem rarely affects the slow bowler, however. More important than anything for this type of bowler

E

to remember is that if he is being hit repeatedly to all parts of the ground by an aggressive batsman, he must keep plugging away, in the hope that he will 'buy' a wicket or two. This is a most difficult thing to do. Too many slow bowlers are so distressed at the thought of their fast deteriorating averages, that they lose all control of length and direction, and give even more runs away. Yet a genuine tactic, when a batsman is carrying all before him, is to introduce a slow bowler into the attack to try to 'buy' his wicket.

So field setting for these types of bowler, the off-spinner, the leg-break and googly bowler, the slow left-arm orthodox spinner and the slow left-arm and chinaman bowler must necessarily be flexible.

I will deal first with the off-spin bowler, and his problems, since this type of bowling has recently become more popular in first-class cricket than the leg-break and googly variety. The latter has momentarily passed out of favour which is, perhaps, another reason why first-class cricket has tended to become duller to watch.

The off-break is bowled with the fingers of the right hand across the seam, the first and second fingers being wide apart to impart the spin as the arm comes over. At the moment of delivery the ball is spun by a movement, a flicking of the fingers to the right, so that it will spin in from the off on landing.

Bowled on a length, on a line of the off stump, the off-break is a very difficult ball to force away, and on good wickets, this is how the ball should be bowled, to a field predominantly an off-side one. That is to say there should be a deep point, cover point and extra cover, and a mid-off in front of the wicket or square to it, a slip and deep backward point behind the wicket.

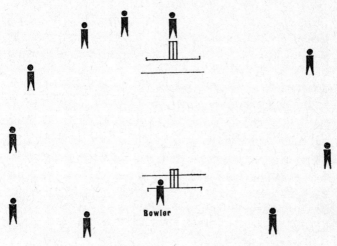

Field for slow left-arm bowler on a turning wicket

On the leg-side there would be only three men – square leg, mid-wicket and mid-on. But if the bowler concerned loses length and direction, and is being hit on the leg-side, the cover point should be moved across to mid-wicket, and the mid-wicket sent to deep square leg on the boundary.

On a turning wicket, the extra cover is dispensed with to pack the leg-side. This allows a leg slip or backward short leg, forward short leg, two men in and around mid-wicket, and a mid-on. If the batsman is attempting to sweep, and getting away with it, mid-wicket must be moved back to deep square leg.

The leg-break is spun with the wrist, and is referred to as wrist spin, rather than finger spin, as off-spin is

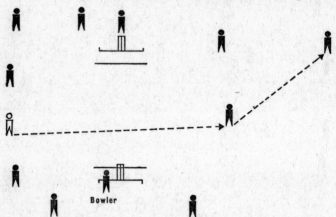

Field for right-arm off-break bowler on a good wicket. If he is being hit on the leg side move cover point across to mid-wicket, and mid-wicket back to deep square leg

described. The wrist is flicked at the batsman at the moment of delivery to impart the spin. Once again the seam is gripped by the fingers, to help them to roll out the ball with a decisive flick that ensures the spin. The top-spinner is a variation of this type of ball – as the name implies making the ball spin straight on instead of turning from leg. The googly, as I have said before, is bowled by letting the ball go out of the back of the hand, thus imparting off spin with a leg break action.

On a good wicket, the leg-break should be aimed at the off or off and middle stumps, and on a turning wicket at the leg or leg and middle. The field for this

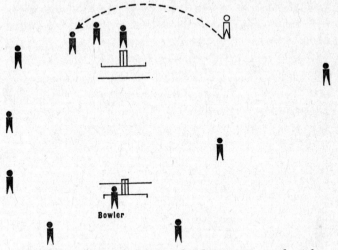

Field for a leg-break bowler, bowling on a good wicket. Backward square leg moves to gully on a wicket taking spin

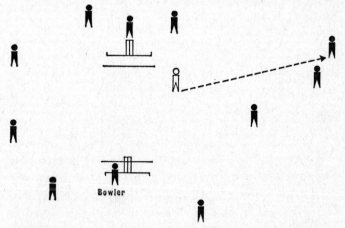

Field for right-arm off-break bowler on a turning wicket. If he is being swept, mid-wicket is moved to deep square leg

type of bowling demands five men on the off-side when the wicket is a favourable one for the batsman, with a sixth man coming across should the ball turn, and favour the bowler. Ordinarily, however, there should be a slip, backward point, cover point, extra cover and mid-off, with a backward square leg, a deep square leg, a mid-wicket and mid-on on the leg side. When the wicket is taking spin, it is advisable to move the backward square leg across to field at short gully.

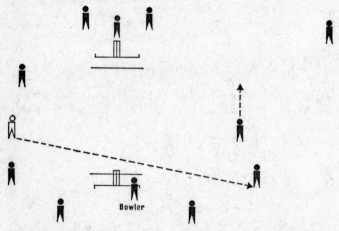

Field for slow left-arm bowler bowling chinamen and googlies
Cover point moves to mid-wicket on a turning wicket

The orthodox left-arm spin bowler bowls what is a leg-break to a right-handed batsman, the chinaman being the left-arm spinner's off-break. The orthodox left-arm spinner should concentrate his attack on the middle and off stumps, or outside them, to a predominantly off-side field consisting of slip, short third man, cover, cover point, extra cover and mid-off. On the leg-side there is just a backward square leg, mid-wicket and mid-on.

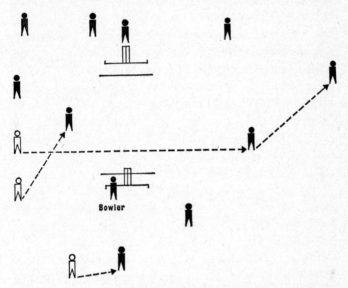

Field for slow left-arm bowler on a good wicket. If he is pitching short, cover point must be moved across to mid-wicket. If he is giving the ball plenty of air, and flighting it well, extra cover can come in to short extra for the possible mis-hit. If he is being hit, mid-off falls back for the hit over the bowler's head

But if the bowler is inclined to pitch the ball short, it will be necessary to move cover point across to mid-wicket, and drop the mid-wicket back to square leg on the boundary. If, however, the bowler is giving the ball plenty of air, and is pitching it accurately, it is advisable to move extra cover in to short extra for the mis-hit, and drop mid-off back to deep mid-off or long-off.

On a turning wicket, the field should be even more packed on the off-side, with slip, gully, cover, cover point, extra cover and mid-off making things very difficult for the batsman to score on this side of the wicket. Just the backward square leg, mid-wicket and mid-on are retained on the leg-side. The line of attack should now be switched to the leg stump or leg and middle on this type of wicket – favouring the bowler. This type of bowler almost always operates round the wicket.

The slow left-arm spin bowler using the chinaman and googly should bowl over the wicket, particularly on a good one, and attempt to bowl on the middle stump, or at middle and off. His field will take in a slip, cover, cover point, extra cover and mid-off on the off-side, a leg slip or backward short leg, deep square leg, mid-wicket and mid-on on the leg-side. On a turning wicket, the attack should be concentrated on the batsman's middle stump, and the cover point can then be moved across the deep mid-wicket, with the mid-wicket moving squarer.

I have illustrated all these field placings with diagrams which should be committed to memory by captains, and by each type of bowler who is anxious to keep down the run rate instead of distributing his fielders at regular intervals round the field, in the hope that they will be in the right place at the right time. Obviously, field settings can be changed to meet the needs of the situation – to combat the tactics of the batsman. But you will not go far wrong if you obey these general principles.

Much can be learned from watching the great bowlers in action, especially if you can beg, borrow or buy a good pair of binoculars, and try to get behind the bowler, near the sight screen. In this way you can really see what he is doing with the ball, and trying to do. The best bowlers I have ever faced were the West Indian pair, and there can't have been many better pairs of opening bowlers in the history of the game. For sheer pace, there is nothing to equal Wes Hall in the world today, and for variation of pace, hostility, and that superb in-swinging yorker, Griffith is out on his own.

Seam bowling, which is the most popular type of bowling in first-class cricket at the moment, possibly to the detriment of the game, has many fine exponents. But the best I have faced are Derek Shackleton, the veteran Hampshire man who is still one of the leading wicket takers, even is his hair is grey and he is forty years of age, Les Jackson of Derbyshire, now retired, and Brian Statham, the great Lancashire bowler.

The leading exponents of off-spin I have faced are John Mortimore, Fred Titmus and David Allen, but there are not many leg-spinners about, because they have taken off the covers again, and the wickets are getting softer. Tony Lock, now in Australia, was the greatest left-arm spinner I've faced during my none too long career, but Doug Slade and Norman Gifford are the pick of the present crop of practitioners.

Watch any of these men performing, and you cannot help but learn plenty.

CHAPTER SIX

SELECTING THE RIGHT EQUIPMENT

Nothing is worse than a good cricket team who look like a motley collection of house painters when they take the field. I am all for having equipment for the game that is comfortable, because there is little point in dressing-up for cricket like a dog's dinner, if you are in agony or a state of acute discomfort for most of the long day that you may be required to spend in the field, or with luck, at the wicket. The happy medium to be struggled for is to be smart and comfortable at all times.

Even in first-class cricket, where one expects this kind of thing to be taboo, runs are given away by both batsman and fielders because the studs in their boots have either worn out or fallen out, or were never there at all. Skating is no part of cricket.

Boots are made out of buckskin, obviously very expensive, and canvas. Buckskin boots are heavier and stiffer initially, but they are bound to last considerably longer, and undoubtedly give far more support to the ankles. Whichever type you choose to buy, or your finances force you to buy, make sure your boots are comfortable. And they must always be white. Any form of whitener will do, and there are scores on the market

74

– creams, liquids, blocks, and so on.

The same applies to your pads, which must not be too large, if you are to be agile between the wickets. Of course, they are useless if they are too small, giving far too little protection to the thighs, which are so vulnerable to the lifting ball. Pads to cover them, and other parts of the body, are now readily available, however – but in my day were not considered necessary in schoolboy cricket.

What is necessary, and absolutely essential for schoolboys, is the best box or protector that money can buy. Even if you have to borrow a bat, buy yourself a box before playing in the nets or your first innings.

The point to remember when buying your bat is that the biggest and heaviest will not necessarily hit the ball furthest and hardest. This is up to the batsman. And if a boy has a bat that is too long for him, he will be struggling to make a stroke without stabbing himself in the stomach, or taking a large divot out of the pitch, for which his team-mates and opponents will hardly thank him. Just as surely the boy with a bat too heavy for him will hardly be in the position to play his aggressive strokes to the bad balls, because the effort of lifting and swinging the bat will be so great that the ball will be long gone before he gets himself into position. I still favour a light bat, so that I can wield it easily, and really get behind the ball and play the strokes.

Always ask for expert advice on the subject of bat buying, and don't be persuaded that a size bigger in bats will last you longer. There is only one size for you – the

right one. Don't buy cheap bats, which are plainly in-
ferior either, in the thought that you are getting a
bargain. A cheap bat is likely to disintegrate far faster
than its more expensive counterpart, unless you are
downright unlucky, and a class bat will strike the ball
far more sweetly.

Buy the best bat that you can afford, and look after it.
Try to oil it regularly with linseed oil, not to saturate
the blade, which will make it soft. Common sense will
tell you how much to use. The length of the handle is
all a matter of preference. Choose the bat handle that
is most comfortable for you – never one that you can
scarcely get a grip on – because it is too thick.

Another essential item of equipment is batting
gloves. Never go to the wicket without them. Hands and
fingers can be hurt easily enough without running the
risk of exposing them to the bowler. Batting gloves
should give you confidence, if you are lacking it, to
stand up to the fast bowlers.

Opinions differ as to the best type of glove to use, but
I favour the sausage type of glove myself. This is a
proper glove, not the kind of thing that you wind round
your hand with elastic, with a sausage-shaped pad on
the back of every finger, and both thumbs. In my
opinion, this type of glove gives the greatest protection.
Some people prefer the type of glove with pieces of
spiky rubber sewn to the back of each finger, but I have
found that this type is not as efficient as the other.
Others say that the type of glove that is not really a
glove, but a succession of finger stalls bound up with
elastic, is the best, because you can feel the bat handle

against the palm of your hand. I have found this no advantage at all – in fact a distinct disadvantage when you are unlucky enough to catch the ball on the splice or at the bottom of the bat – and get stung.

The wearing of a cap also depends on the individual's choice. Some like them, others not. Officials will tell you to wear a cap and you will not miss any catches, but this is nonsense. A cap is no protection against the sun when you are looking right up into it – trying to find the ball that has been skied. But a good cap, with a reasonably long peak – a short peak is useless – does stop the glare when the weather is particularly bright. I find one invaluable for this, fielding as I do in the slips, and a cap is indispensable to most players who are unfortunate enough to have to wear spectacles – Mike Smith is seldom seen without one.

Gaberdine flannels are not too expensive, and hang nicely. Never be persuaded to get yourself decked out in a pair of thin, tapering trousers, because you will find that you are unable to bend quickly in this type without risking an accident, and mobility is essential in all departments of the game. If you can afford them, then it is advantageous to have two pairs – one for batting – another for fielding. A change is as good as a rest, and this also applies to socks.

Do not be persuaded to buy nylon shirts, or shirts made of other man-made fabrics, unless you are sure they are able to breathe properly. Otherwise you will find yourself in a lather of sweat from the first moment you exert yourself. These are garments used by slimmers. Unless you are over-weight, leave them alone! There is nothing to beat a good quality, hard-wearing cotton poplin.

Wicket-keepers, being a race apart, are especially catered for with wide pads, and special gloves. I have only one word of advice for this breed – wear inner gloves. There is nothing soft about wearing them, and however slow or fast is the bowler, he can still knock your hands up. Any extra little bit of protection available should be snapped up. After all, you are not making your living at the game – yet – and when you are, and your livelihood depends on your keeping fit to play, protection is just as important.

CHAPTER SEVEN

THE LANGUAGE OF THE GAME

Cricket has a language all of its own, and to help new-comers to the game I have outlined a few of the terms and their meanings, to help sort out what can be a complicated jargon to the uninitiated.

Abandon: used of a game that has already been affected – usually by weather. When there is no hope of a result, the game is abandoned.

Analysis: details of a bowler's figures, including overs bowled, number of maidens bowled, runs scored off him, and wickets taken.

Appeal: the cry of 'how is that?' or something similar, appealing to an umpire for a wicket – i.e. run out, or caught at the wicket.

Average: the number of runs scored by a batsman is divided by the number of his completed innings – uncompleted innings not being counted – to arrive at a batting average; the number of runs scored off his bowling is divided by the number of wickets taken to arrive at a bowling average.

Back up: to move into position at a throw in so that if the man at the stumps fails to catch the ball, the man backing up does so; a batsman at the bowler's end

backs up by moving out of his crease in preparation
for a run.

Bail: the piece of wood, $4\frac{5}{8}$ inches in length, that rests
in the grooves on the top of the stumps, and must be
dislodged before a batsman can be bowled out, run
out or stumped. There are two to each wicket.

Ball: the regulation size measures between $8\frac{13}{16}$ and nine
inches in circumference, and weighs between $5\frac{1}{2}$ and
$5\frac{3}{4}$ oz.

Bat: made of willow, and must not measure more than
$4\frac{1}{4}$ inches in width and 38 inches in length.

Beamer: a ball aimed at the batsman's head, without
bouncing.

Blade: the part of the bat used to hit the ball.

Block: to play the ball defensively, rather than try to
score; blockhole being the mark made by the batsman
when taking guard on or around the popping crease.

Bouncer: also known as bumper; short pitched fast ball
that rears up sharply off the pitch.

Boundary: the limit of the field; if the batsman hits the
ball over the boundary without a bounce, he is
credited with six runs; four if the ball bounces before
reaching the boundary.

Bowl unchanged: to bowl throughout an innings.

Bump ball: a ball that appears to be caught by the fielder,
but has in fact touched the ground after being hit.

Bye: a run scored without the ball having been hit,
usually scored because the wicket-keeper fails to take
the ball.

Carry bat: an opening batsman does so by being not out
when the innings closes.

The 'broken' wrist that caused so much no-ball trouble for Tony Lock, the
Surrey and England left arm spin bowler, now playing in Australian State
cricket

The action that helped Lock to keep out of trouble with the umpires. Note that
the wrist is stiff

Caught and bowled: meaning that the bowler takes a catch off his own bowling.

Caught sub: meaning that the batsman has been caught by a substitute fielder.

Century: one hundred runs or over scored by one batsman; thus **Double century** means over 200 runs.

Century stand: a total of 100 runs made by two batsmen in a partnership.

Chance: possibility of dismissing the batsman – caught, stumped, run out, etc.

Change: to introduce a new bowler.

Change bowler: a useful bowler who can be used when the opening bowlers are rested.

Change ends: used of bowlers, who are tried at different ends in turn.

Chinaman: a left arm bowler's off-break.

Clean bowled: batsman bowled out – completely beaten by ball.

Close field: those fielders in positions close to the wicket.

Closure: usually used after a declaration, indicating the end of an innings.

Collapse: quick dismissal of several batsmen.

Covers : that part of the field in the region of cover-point on the off-side. Also materials used for protecting the pitch from the weather.

Creeper: ball that keeps low after bouncing.

Crumble: a term used to describe a pitch that is cracking up.

Cutters: type of delivery that appears to cut off the pitch in same direction as it is swerving in flight.

Cut up: describes pitch roughed up by use, and by

bowlers' follow through, and stud marks.

Dead bat: technique of stunning the dangerous ball, bringing it down in front of the batsman and avoiding giving a catch to a close fielder.

Dead ball: a ball not in play.

Dead wicket: a pitch on which there is little bounce, and the ball appears to be slowed on bouncing.

Declaration: the closure of an innings when the total is considered sufficient, and not all the batsmen have had an innings.

Deep: used to describe the fielding positions far from the wicket.

Defensive stroke or bowling: stroke intended to protect wicket rather than score: defensive bowling to keep down rate of scoring is usually wide of the stumps or just short of a length.

Draw: result of match that is unfinished at the close, i.e. neither side has lost nor won.

Draw stumps: to end the day's play.

Duck: a score of nothing.

Easy paced: of a pitch; when the ball does not come up sharply.

Extras: runs credited to a team rather than to an individual for fielding and bowling errors – byes, leg byes, wides, no balls.

Fall of a wicket: a batsman is out, no matter how.

First wicket down: used of the number three batsman who goes in on the fall of the first wicket.

Flight: the movement of the ball in the air when bowled.

Full pitch or full toss: the delivery that is struck by the batsman before it has a chance to pitch.

Get off the mark: score first run.

Get up: of a ball that gets up sharply off the pitch.

Googly: off-break with a leg-break action.

Guard: position of bat in relation to stumps as seen by the umpire and bowler at the other end of the pitch.

Half-volley: ball struck by the bat as it pitches.

Hat trick: a bowler takes three wickets with consecutive balls – can be last two of one innings – first ball of next.

'How's that?': the traditional appeal for a dismissal in cricket.

Hit wicket: batsman gets himself out by striking his own stumps in the act of playing a stroke.

Innings: the batting performance of a team or player.

Inside edge: the edge of the bat nearest to the batsman.

Keep end up: to bat slowly but surely while your partner does most of the scoring.

Knock: popular name for innings of a batsman.

L.B.W.: abbreviation for leg before wicket.

Lead: the number of runs by which one team's total exceeds that of their opponents.

Leave: a ball leaves the batsman if it goes away to the off, either outswinging or breaking from leg. Let a ball go past the stumps without making any attempt to play at it.

Leg before wicket: a batsman is out in this way if he is struck by a ball that is pitched on the line of the stumps, and in the opinion of the umpire at the bowler's end, would have gone on to hit the wicket had not the batsman's body or legs intervened.

Leg-break: ball spun from leg to off.

Leg-bye: runs earned by a side when a ball strikes any part of the batsman's body if, in the umpire's opinion, he is attempting to play a stroke, and the ball evades fielders or wicket-keeper.

Leg theory: the tactics of bowling down the leg-side to a packed leg-side field.

Life: a batsman is given a life if a catch is dropped thus allowing him to continue batting.

Loft: to lift the ball into the outfield.

Long handle: expression used to denote hard hitting, because the batsman grips the handle near its end to get the maximum swing.

Long hop: a short pitched ball that is easily hit by the batsman.

Maiden: a maiden over is an over in which the batsman is unable to score.

Misfield: to fail to stop a ball hit by a batsman in your direction.

Miss: usually used of fielders when missing a catch.

New ball: this is used at the start of each innings, and another can be used when the batting side has reached 200 runs, or the fielding side has got through 85 overs in first class cricket.

Nip-Backer: Ball that swings one way and breaks back the other off the seam.

No ball: so called by the umpire when a bowler infringes on the laws regarding creases, or throws, etc. A batsman may only be run out off a no ball. If he fails to score off it, the no ball counts as an extra run to his side. If he does score, the no ball does not count, and his runs are credited to the batsman.

Not out: declaration by an umpire in rejecting an appeal; also one man's innings of the eleven must finish this way – only ten wickets can fall so someone remains not out.

Off-break: a ball spun from off to leg.

Off the mark: batsman opens his score.

Open account: to begin scoring.

Opening pair: the batsmen who open the innings for their side – can be called openers.

Opening stand: a stand or partnership involving the opening batsmen.

Out cricket: used to describe the work of the fielding side.

Out of ground: a batsman is out of his ground when he strays beyond the popping crease, or has not reached the popping crease at the other end when running.

Outside edge: the edge of the bat further from the batsman.

Over: six balls bowled by the bowler before the other bowler takes over for an over at the other end. Eight balls to an over in Australia.

Overbowl: to bowl a man for too long in one spell.

Over pitch: to bowl a ball of too full length so that the batsman can strike it before it touches the ground.

Over the wicket: to bowl with the arm nearer to the stumps.

Overthrow: a run taken when a throw in to the wicket is inaccurate enough to allow this.

Pace: the speed of the ball – in the air or off the pitch.

Pad up: to take the ball deliberately on the pads.

Pair (of spectacles): refers to two ducks in one match –

a batsman out without scoring in either innings.

Partner: the other batsman of the pair at the wicket.

Partnership: the number of runs earned by two batsmen at the wicket together.

'Play': an order by the umpire to commence bowling at the start of an innings.

Play on: to get out by striking the ball on to one's own wicket.

Plumb: said of a perfect batting wicket.

Popping crease: a line parallel to the bowling crease and four feet in front of it.

Pop up: description of ball that jumps up on pitching.

Put in: asked to bat by the opposing captain.

Put on: asked to bowl by your captain.

Retired hurt: a batsman who temporarily postpones his innings because of injury, sustained during it.

Return catch: a catch taken by the bowler.

Round arm: to deliver the ball with the arm at shoulder height.

Round the wicket: in this position the bowler's arm is further from the wicket.

Run out: to trap a batsman by breaking the wicket before he has gained his crease.

Run up: refers to the bowler's approach before delivery.

Seam: raised band round ball, helpful to bowler's grip.

Seam bowler: one who uses the seam to swing the ball, and turn it off the pitch.

Shooter: a ball that does not rise off the pitch on landing.

Short run: disallowed run because the batsman has not reached the popping crease at the other end of the pitch before starting on another run.

Sight screens: large screens of white-painted boards or sheets placed behind the wicket at both ends of the ground to provide a background that enables the batsman to see the ball leaving the bowler's hand.

Single: one run.

Sitter: an easy catch.

Skier: a ball hit high in the air, giving a catch.

Snick: a false, edged stroke.

Splice: V-shaped joint between the handle and blade of the bat.

Square leg umpire: one umpire always stands in this position when the bowling is from the other end of the pitch.

Stance: position adopted by the batsman.

Sticky: refers to state of wicket drying out after rain, and taking considerable amount of spin.

Stock bowler: reliable bowler for long spells.

Stonewall: to bat defensively.

Substitute or sub: player allowed to field only when one of his own side is injured, but not to bat or bowl.

Swing: to move the ball either way in the air.

Tail end: the last few players in a side – the poorest batsmen.

Take off: to end a bowler's spell.

Thrown out: the loss of a wicket caused by a throw that hits the stumps to run out a batsman.

Tie: different from a drawn game in that the scores of each side end level, after a full innings by each.

Tight bowling: bowling which makes scoring difficult – of good length and direction.

Top spin: spin that causes the ball to hurry straight on.

Toss: the toss of a coin which enables the captain who wins it to choose whether his side shall bat or field.

Trimmer: a ball which just removes the bails without disturbing the stumps.

Turn: to spin the ball.

Turning wicket: wicket that is taking considerable spin.

Umpires: the two officials who control the game.

Wicket: consists of three stumps 28 inches high, and spaced to be nine inches in overall width. Wickets are set 22 yards apart.

Wickets in hand: those of batsmen still to bat.

Wide: bowled so far from batsman's reach that the bowler is penalised one run – an extra.

Wrong un: the googly is so described.

Yorker: a ball of full length that passes under the bat of the batsman as he gropes forward.

These are but a few of the simplest terms and phrases used in the game. I have omitted the fielding positions, which are more easily learned off the diagram, and the types of stroke, which are also charted. Cricket has much more slang, or language of common usage, than it is possible to list here. Nor would it be possible to deal with the question of tactics without devoting an entire book to the subject. Such are the complications and the delights of this wonderful English game. I hope this book will make a sweet science a little easier to understand for some of its newest recruits, and perhaps further the enjoyment of some who have never been taught the finer points.

CHAPTER EIGHT

THE LAWS OF CRICKET
(Reproduced by courtesy of the
Marylebone Cricket Club)

PREFACE

During the last two hundred years the conduct of the game of Cricket has been governed by a series of Codes of Laws. These Codes were established as indicated below, and were at all times subject to additions and alterations ordained by the governing authorities of the time. Since its formation in 1787 the Marylebone Cricket Club has been recognised as the sole authority for drawing up the Code and for all subsequent alterations.

There is little doubt that Cricket was subject to recognised rules as early as 1700, though the earliest known Code is that drawn up in 1744 by certain Noblemen and Gentlemen who used the Artillery Ground in London. These Laws were revised in 1755 by 'Several Cricket-Clubs, particularly that of the Star and Garter in Pall-Mall.'

The next arrangement was produced by 'a Committee of Noblemen and Gentlemen of Kent, Hampshire, Surrey, Sussex, Middlesex and London,' at the Star and

Garter on February 25th, 1774, and this in turn was revised by a similar body in February, 1786.

On May 30th, 1788, the first M.C.C. Code was adopted, and remained in force until May 19th, 1835, when a new Code of Laws was approved by the Committee. The Laws appear to have been first numbered in 1823.

The 1835 Code, amended in detail from time to time, stood until April 21st, 1884, when, after consultation with cricket clubs both at home and overseas, important alterations were incorporated in a new version adopted at a Special General Meeting of the M.C.C.

By 1939, these Laws supplemented as they had been by the inclusion of many definitions and interpretations in the form of notes, were in need of revision, and immediately on the conclusion of the World War the opinions of controlling Bodies and Clubs throughout the world were sought, with the result that the present code was adopted at a Special General Meeting of the M.C.C. on May 7th, 1947.

This revision in the main aimed at the clarification and better arrangement of the previous Laws and their interpretations, but did not exclude certain definite alterations designed firstly to provide greater latitude in the conduct of the game as required by the widely differing conditions in which it is played, and secondly to eliminate certain umpiring difficulties.

This, the third edition of the 1947 Code, contains a few small alterations to the Laws and certain alterations and amendments to the Notes published since 1952.

Under the Rules of the Marylebone Cricket Club the

Laws of Cricket can only be changed by the vote of two-thirds of the members present and voting at a Special General Meeting, of which due notice is required to be given.

From time to time the Committee of the M.C.C. are required to give interpretations on points of difficulty arising from the Laws, and these are given in the form of notes to the Laws themselves.

The primary purpose of the book as expressed by the late Sir Francis Lacey (Secretary of the M.C.C. from 1898 to 1926) remains unchanged:

'The aim of this publication is to remove difficulties, which are known to exist, although they are not always apparent. Hundreds of cases are sent to the M.C.C. for decision every year. It is from this source that the chief difficulties have become manifest. Saturday and League Matches are especially productive of disputes, and it is hoped that those who read these notes may find an answer to any doubt which may arise as to the proper interpretation of the Laws of Cricket.'

Lord's Cricket Ground,
London, N.W.8.   R. AIRD,
1st July, 1962   Secretary, M.C.C.

(A) – THE PLAYERS, UMPIRES AND SCORERS

SIDES

1. A match is played between two sides of eleven players each, unless otherwise agreed. Each side shall play under a Captain who before the toss for innings shall

nominate his players who may not thereafter be changed without the consent of the opposing Captain.

NOTES

1. If a captain is not available at any time, a deputy must act for him to deal promptly with points arising from this and other Laws.

2. No match in which more than eleven players a side take part can be regarded as First-class, and in any case no side should field with more than eleven players.

SUBSTITUTES

2. Substitute shall be allowed to field or run between the wickets for any player who may during the match be incapacitated from illness or injury, but not for any other reason without the consent of the opposing Captain; no Substitute shall be allowed to bat or bowl. Consent as to the person to act as substitute in the field shall be obtained from the opposing Captain, who may indicate positions in which the Substitute shall not field.

NOTES

1. A player may bat, bowl or field even though a substitute has acted for him previously.

2. An injured batsman may be 'Out' should his runner infringe Laws 36, 40 or 41. As *Striker* he remains himself subject to the Laws; should he be out of his ground for any purpose he may be 'Out' under Laws 41 and 42 at the wicket-keeper's end, irrespective of the position of the other batsman or the substitute when the wicket is put down. When *not the Striker* the

injured batsman is out of the game and stands where he does not interfere with the play.

THE APPOINTMENT OF UMPIRES

3. Before the toss for innings two Umpires shall be appointed, one for each end to control the game as required by the Laws with absolute impartiality. No Umpire shall be changed during a match without the consent of both Captains.

NOTE

1. The umpires should report themselves to the executive of the ground 30 minutes before the start of each day's play.

THE SCORERS

4. All runs scored shall be recorded by Scorers appointed for the purpose; the Scorers shall accept and acknowledge all instructions and signals given to them by the Umpires.

NOTE

1. The umpires should wait until a signal has been answered by a scorer before allowing the game to proceed. Mutual consultation between the scorers and the umpires to clear up doubtful points is at all times permissible.

(B) – THE IMPLEMENTS OF THE GAME, AND THE GROUND

THE BALL

5. The Ball shall weigh not less than 5½ ounces, nor

more than $5\frac{3}{4}$ ounces. It shall measure not less than $8\frac{13}{16}$ inches, nor more than 9 inches in circumference. Subject to agreement to the contrary either Captain may demand a new ball at the start of each innings. In the event of a ball being lost or becoming unfit for play, the Umpires shall allow another ball to be taken into use. They shall inform the Batsmen whenever a ball is to be changed.

NOTES

1. All cricket balls used in First-class matches should be approved before the start of a match by the umpires and captains.

2. Except in the United Kingdom, or if local regulations provide otherwise, after 200 runs have been made off a ball in First-class matches, the captain of the fielding side may demand a new one. In First-class matches in the United Kingdom the fielding side may demand a new ball after 65 (6 ball) overs have been bowled with the old one. In other grades of cricket these regulations will not apply unless agreed before the toss for innings.

3. Any ball substituted for one lost or becoming unfit for play should have had similar wear or use as that of the one discarded.

THE BAT

6. The Bat shall not exceed $4\frac{1}{4}$ inches in the widest part; it shall not be more than 38 inches in length.

THE PITCH

7. The Pitch is deemed to be the area of ground between the bowling creases, 5 feet in width on either side

of the line joining the centre of the wickets. Before the toss for innings, the executive of the ground shall be responsible for the selection and preparation of the Pitch; thereafter the Umpires shall control its use and maintenance. The Pitch shall not be changed during a match unless it becomes unfit for play, and then only with the consent of both Captains.

THE WICKETS

8. The Wickets shall be pitched opposite and parallel to each other at a distance of 22 yards from stump to stump. Each Wicket shall be 9 inches in width and consist of three stumps with two bails upon the top. The stumps shall be of equal and of sufficient size to prevent the ball from passing through, with their top 28 inches above the ground. The bails shall be each $4\frac{3}{8}$ inches in length, and, when in position on the top of the stumps, shall not project more than $\frac{1}{2}$ inch above them.

NOTES

1. Except for the bail grooves the tops of the stumps shall be dome-shaped.

2. In a high wind the captains may agree, with the approval of the umpires, to dispense with the use of bails (*see* Law 31, Note 3).

THE BOWLING AND POPPING CREASES

9. The bowling crease shall be in line with the stumps; 8 feet 8 inches in length; the stumps in the centre; with a Return crease at each end at right angles behind the wicket. The Popping crease shall be marked 4 feet in front of and parallel with the Bowling crease. Both the

Return and Popping creases shall be deemed unlimited in length.

1. The distance of the Popping Crease from the wicket is measured from a line running through the centre of the stumps to the inside edge of the crease.

(C) – THE CARE AND MAINTENANCE OF THE PITCH

ROLLING, MOWING AND WATERING

10. Unless permitted by special regulations, the Pitch shall not be rolled during a match except before the start of each innings and of each day's play, when, if the Captain of the batting side so elect, it may be swept and rolled for not more than 7 minutes. The Pitch shall not be mown during a match unless special regulations so provide. Under no circumstances shall the Pitch be watered during a match.

NOTES

1. 'Special Regulations', within the framework of the Laws, referred to in this and subsequent Laws are those authorised by M.C.C. in respect of County Cricket, or by Overseas Governing Bodies in respect of cricket in the countries concerned. Such Regulations do not apply to matches played by touring teams unless included in these Notes and Interpretations of the Official Laws, or unless agreed to by both parties before the visiting team arrives.

2. The umpires are responsible that any rolling per-

Norman O'Neill, the exciting
Australian batsman,
demonstrates a thrilling shot –
the pull. The batsman is on
tiptoe as he gets his full power
behind the shot. His eye has
never left the rising ball

orman O'Neill hooks the
ll high to the boundary

Freddie Trueman accelerates as he approaches the wicket to bowl

Compare Trueman's action with that of Lindwall – the left shoulder pointing at the batsman – body arched backwards

mitted by this Law and carried out at the request of the captain of the batting side, is in accordance with the regulations laid down and that it is completed so as to allow play to start at the stipulated time.

The normal rolling before the start of each day's play shall take place not earlier than half an hour before the start of play, but the captain of the batting side may delay such rolling until 10 minutes before the start of play should he so desire.

3. The time allowed for rolling shall be taken out of the normal playing time if a captain declare an innings closed either, (*a*) before play starts on any day so late that the other captain is prevented from exercising his option in regard to rolling under this Law, or (*b*) during the luncheon interval later than 15 minutes after the start of such interval.

4. Except in the United Kingdom, if at any time a rain affected pitch is damaged by play thereon, it shall be swept and rolled for a period of not more than ten consecutive minutes at any time between the close of play on the day on which it was damaged and the next resumption of play, provided that:

    (i) The umpires shall instruct the groundsman to sweep and roll the pitch only after they have agreed that damage caused to it as a result of play after rain has fallen warrants such rolling additional to that provided for in Law 10.

    (ii) Such rolling shall in all cases be done under the personal supervision of both umpires and shall take place at such time and with such roller as the groundsman shall consider best calculated to repair the damage to the pitch.

(iii) Not more than one such additional rolling shall be permitted as a result of rain on any particular day.

(iv) The rolling provided for in Law 10, to take place before the start of play, shall not be permitted on any day on which the rolling herein provided for takes place within two hours of the time appointed for commencement of play on that day.

5. The pitch shall be mown under the supervision of the umpires before play begins on alternate days after the start of a match, but should the pitch not be so mown on any day on account of play not taking place, it shall be mown on the first day on which the match is resumed and thereafter on alternate days. (For the purpose of this rule a rest day counts as a day.)

COVERING THE PITCH

11. The Pitch shall not be completely covered during a match unless special regulations so provide; covers used to protect the bowlers' run up shall not extend to a greater distance than 3½ feet in front of the Popping creases.

NOTE

1. It is usual under this Law to protect the bowlers' run up, before and during a match, both at night and, when necessary, during the day. The covers should be removed early each morning, if fine.

MAINTENANCE OF THE PITCH

12. The Batsman may beat the Pitch with his bat, and

Players may secure their footholds by the use of sawdust, provided Law 46 be not thereby contravened. In wet weather the Umpires shall see that the holes made by the Bowlers and Batsmen are cleaned out and dried whenever necessary to facilitate play.

(D) – THE CONDUCT OF THE GAME

INNINGS

13. Each side has two innings, taken alternately, except in the case provided for in Law 14. The choice of innings shall be decided by tossing on the field of play.

NOTES

1. The captains should toss for innings not later than 15 minutes before the time agreed upon for play to start. The winner of the toss may not alter his decision to bat or field once it has been notified to the opposing captain.

2. This Law also governs a One-day match in which play continues after the completion of the first innings of both sides. (*See also* Law 22.)

FOLLOWING INNINGS

14. The side which bats first and leads by 150 runs in a match of three days or more, by 100 runs in a two-day match, or by 75 runs in a one-day match, shall have the option of requiring the other side to follow their innings.

DECLARATIONS

15. The Captain of the batting side may declare an

innings closed at any time during a match irrespective of its duration.

16. When the start of play is delayed by weather Law 14 shall apply in accordance with the number of days' play remaining from the actual start of the match.

START AND CLOSE OF PLAY AND INTERVALS

17. The Umpires shall allow such intervals as have been agreed upon for meals, 10 minutes between each innings and not more than 2 minutes for each fresh batsman to come in. At the start of each innings and of each day's play and at the end of any interval the Umpire at the Bowler's end shall call 'Play', when the side refusing to play shall lose the match. After 'Play' has been called no trial ball shall be allowed to any player, and when one of the Batsmen is out the use of the bat shall not be allowed to any player until the next Batsman shall come in.

NOTES

1. The umpires shall not award a match under this Law unless (i) 'Play' has been called in such a manner that both sides can clearly understand that play is to start, (ii) an appeal has been made, and (iii) they are satisfied that a side will not, or cannot, continue play.

2. It is an essential duty of the captains to ensure that the 'ingoing' batsman passes the 'out-coming' one before the latter leaves the field of play. This is all the more important in view of the responsibility resting on the umpires for deciding whether or not the delay of the individual amounts to a refusal of the batting side to continue play.

3. The interval for luncheon should not exceed 45 minutes unless otherwise agreed (but *see* Law 10, Note 3). In the event of the last wicket falling within 2 minutes of the time arranged for luncheon or tea, the game shall be resumed at the usual hour, no allowance being made for the 10 minutes between the innings.

4. Bowling practice *on the pitch* is forbidden at any time during the game.

18. The Umpires shall call 'Time', and at the same time remove the bails from both wickets, on the cessation of play before any arranged interval, at the end of each day's play, and at the conclusion of the match. An 'Over' shall always be started if 'Time' has not been reached, and shall be completed unless a batsman is 'Out' or 'Retires' within 2 minutes of the completion of any period of play, but the 'Over' in progress at the close of play on the final day of a match shall be completed at the request of either Captain even if a wicket fall after 'Time' has been reached.

NOTES

1. If, during the completion of the last over of any period of play, the players have occasion to leave the field, the Umpires shall call 'time'. In the case of the last over of the match, there shall be no resumption of play and the match shall be at an end.

2. The last over before an interval or the close of play shall be started, provided the umpire standing at square leg, after walking at his normal pace, has arrived at his position behind the stumps at the bowler's end before time has been reached.

SCORING

19. The score shall be reckoned by runs. A run is scored:

1st. So often as the Batsman after a hit, or at any time while the ball is in play, shall have crossed and made good their ground from end to end; but if either Batsman run a short run, the Umpire shall call and signal 'One short' and that run shall not be scored. The Striker being caught, no run shall be scored; a Batsman being run out, that run which was being attempted shall not be scored.

2nd. For penalties under Laws 21, 27, 29, 44 and boundary allowances under Law 20.

NOTES

1. If while the ball is in play, the batsmen have crossed in running, neither returns to the wicket he has left except in the case of a boundary hit, or a boundary from extras, or under Laws 30 Note 1 and 46 Note 4 (vii). This rule applies even should a short run have been called, or should no run be reckoned as in the case of a catch.

2. A run is 'short' if either, or both, batsmen fail to make good their ground in turning for a further run.

Although such a 'short' run shortens the succeeding one, the latter, if completed, counts. Similarly a batsman taking stance in front of his popping crease may run from that point without penalty.

3. (i) One run only is deducted if both batsmen are short in one and the same run.

(ii) Only if three or more runs are attempted can

more than one run be 'short' and then, subject to (i) above, all runs so called shall be disallowed.

(iii) If either or both batsmen deliberately run short, the umpire is justified in calling 'Dead Ball' and disallowing any runs attempted or scored as soon as he sees that the fielding side have no chance of dismissing either batsman under the Laws.

4. An umpire signals 'short' runs when the ball becomes 'dead' by bending his arm upwards to touch the shoulder with the tips of his fingers. If there has been more than one 'short' run the umpires must instruct the scorers as to the number of runs disallowed. (*See* Note 1 to Law 4.)

BOUNDARIES

20. Before the toss for innings the Umpires shall agree with both sides on the Boundaries for play, and on the allowances to be made for them. An Umpire shall call or signal 'Boundary' whenever, in his opinion, a ball in play hits, crosses or is carried over the Boundary. The runs completed at the instant the ball reaches the Boundary shall count only should they exceed the allowance, but if the 'Boundary' result from an overthrow or from the wilful act of a fieldsman, any runs already made and the allowance shall be added to the score.

NOTES

1. If flags or posts are used to mark a boundary, the real or imaginary line joining such points shall be regarded as the boundary, which should be marked by a white line if possible.

2. In deciding on the allowances to be made for

boundaries the umpires will be guided by the prevailing custom of the ground.

3. It is a 'Boundary' if the ball touches any boundary line or if a fieldsman with ball in hand grounds any part of his person on or over that line. A fieldsman, however, standing with the playing area may lean against or touch a boundary fence in fielding a ball (*see also* Law 35, Note 5).

4. An obstacle, or person, within the playing area is not regarded as a boundary unless so arranged by the umpires. The umpire is not a boundary, but sight screens within the playing area shall be so regarded.

5. The customary allowance for a boundary is 4 runs, but it is usual to allow 6 runs for all hits pitching over and clear of the boundary line or fence (even though the ball has been previously touched by a fieldsman). It is not usual to allow 6 runs when a ball hits a sight screen full pitch, if the latter is on or inside the boundary.

6. In the case of a boundary resulting from either an overthrow or the wilful act of a fieldsman, the run in progress counts provided that the batsmen have crossed at the instant of the throw or act.

7. The umpire signals 'Boundary' by waving an arm from side to side, or a boundary '6' by raising both arms above the head.

LOST BALL

21. If a ball in play cannot be found or recovered any Fieldsman may call 'Lost Ball', when 6 runs shall be added to the score; but if more than 6 have been run before 'Lost Call' be called, as many runs as have been run shall be scored.

THE RESULT

22. A match is won by the side which shall have scored a total of runs in excess of that scored by the opposing side in its two completed innings; one-day matches, unless thus played out, shall be decided by the first innings. A match may also be determined by being given up as lost by one of the sides, or in the case governed by Law 17. A match not determined in any of these ways, shall count as a 'Draw'.

NOTES

1. It is the responsibility of the captains to satisfy themselves on the correctness of the scores on the conclusion of play.

2. Neither side can be compelled to continue after a match is finished; a one-day match shall not be regarded as finished on the result of the first innings if the umpires consider there is a prospect of carrying the game to a further issue in the time remaining.

3. The result of a finished match is stated as a win by runs, except in the case of a win by the side batting last, when it is by the number of wickets still then to fall. In a one-day match which is not played out on the second innings, this rule applies to the position at the time when a result on the first innings was reached.

4. A 'Draw' is regarded as a 'Tie' when the scores are equal at the conclusion of play but only if the match has been played out. If the scores of the completed first innings of a one-day match are equal, it is a 'Tie', but only if the match has not been played out to a further conclusion.

THE OVER

23. The ball shall be bowled from each wicket alternately in Overs of either 8 or 6 balls according to the agreed conditions of play. When the agreed number have been bowled and it has become clear to the Umpire at the Bowler's wicket that both sides have ceased to regard the ball as in play, the Umpire shall call 'Over' in a distinct manner before leaving the wicket. Neither a 'No Ball' nor a 'Wide Ball' shall be reckoned as one of the 'Over'.

NOTE

1. In the United Kingdom the 'over' shall be 6 balls, unless an agreement to the contrary has been made.

24. A Bowler shall finish an 'Over' in progress unless he be incapacitated or be suspended for unfair play. He shall be allowed to change ends as often as desired, provided only that he shall not bowl two 'Overs' consecutively in one innings. A Bowler may require the Batsman at the wicket from which he is bowling to stand on whichever side of it he may direct.

DEAD BALL

25. The ball shall be held to be 'Dead' – on being in the opinion of the Umpire finally settled in the hands of the Wicket-keeper or of the Bowler; or on reaching or pitching over the boundary; or, whether played or not, on lodging in the dress of either a Batsman or Umpire; or on the call of 'Over' or 'Time' by the Umpire; or on a Batsman being out from any cause; or on any penalty being awarded under Laws 21 or 44. The Umpire shall call 'Dead Ball' should he decide to intervene under Law

46 in a case of unfair play or in the event of a serious injury to a player; or should he require to suspend play prior to the Striker receiving a delivery. The ball shall cease to be 'Dead' on the Bowler starting his run or bowling action.

NOTES

1. Whether the ball is 'finally settled' is a question of fact for the umpire alone to decide.

2. An umpire is justified in suspending play prior to the striker receiving a delivery in any of the following circumstances:

   (i) If satisfied that, for an *adequate* reason, the striker is not ready to receive the ball, and makes no attempt to play it.

   (ii) If the bowler drops the ball accidentally before delivery, or if the ball does not leave his hand for any reason.

   (iii) If one or both bails fall from the striker's wicket before he receives the delivery.

In such cases the ball is regarded as 'Dead' from the time it last came into play.

3. A ball does not become 'Dead' when it strikes an umpire (unless it lodges in his dress), when the wicket is broken or struck down (unless a batsman is out thereby), or when an unsuccessful appeal is made.

4. For the purpose of this and other Laws, the term 'dress' includes the equipment and clothing of players and umpires as normally worn.

NO BALL

26. For a delivery to be fair the ball must be bowled,

not thrown or jerked; if either Umpire be not entirely satisfied of the absolute fairness of a delivery in this respect, he shall call and signal 'No Ball' instantly upon delivery. The Umpire at the Bowler's wicket shall call and signal 'No Ball' if he is not satisfied that at the instant of delivery the Bowler has at least some part of one foot behind the Bowling crease and within the Return crease, and not touching or grounded over either crease.

NOTES

1. Subject to the provisions of the Law being complied with a bowler is not debarred from delivering the ball with both feet behind the bowling crease.

2. The striker is entitled to know whether the bowler intends to bowl over or round the wicket, overarm or underarm, right- or left-handed. An umpire may regard any failure to notify a change in the mode of delivery as 'unfair', if so, he should call 'No ball'.

3. It is a 'No Ball' if the bowler before delivering a ball throws it at the striker's wicket even in an attempt to run him out (*see* Law 46, Note 4 (vii)).

4. If a bowler break the near wicket with any part of his person during the delivery, such act in itself does not constitute 'No Ball'.

5. The umpire signals 'No Ball' by extending one arm horizontally.

6. An umpire should revoke the call 'No Ball' if the ball does not leave the bowler's hand for any reason.

27. The ball does not become 'Dead' on the call of 'No Ball'. The Striker may hit a 'No Ball' and whatever

runs result shall be added to his score, but runs made otherwise from a 'No Ball' shall be scored 'No Balls', and if no runs be made one run shall be so scored. The Striker shall be out from a 'No Ball' if he break Law 37, and either Batsman may be run out, or given out if he break Laws 36 or 40.

NOTES

1. The penalty for a 'No Ball' is only scored if no runs result otherwise.

2. Law 46 Note 4 (vii) covers attempts to run before the ball is delivered, but should the non-striker unfairly leave his ground too soon, the fielding side may run out the batsman at the bowler's end by any recognised method. If the bowler throws at the near wicket, the umpire does not call 'No Ball', though any runs resulting are so scored. The throw does not count in the 'Over'.

WIDE BALL

28. If the Bowler shall bowl the ball so high over or so wide of the wicket that in the opinion of the Umpire it passes out of reach of the Striker, and would not have been within his reach when taking guard in the normal position, the Umpire shall call and signal 'Wide Ball' as soon as it shall have passed the Striker.

NOTES

1. If a ball which the umpire considers to have been delivered comes to rest in front of the striker 'Wide' should not be called, and no runs should be added to the score unless they result from the striker hitting the

ball which he has a right to do without interference by the fielding side. Should the fielding side interfere, the umpire is justified in replacing the ball where it came to rest and ordering the fieldsmen to resume the places they occupied in the field before the ball was delivered.

2. The umpire signals 'Wide' by extending both arms horizontally.

3. An umpire should revoke the call if the striker hits a ball which has been called 'Wide'.

29. The ball does not become 'Dead' on the call of 'Wide Ball'. All runs that are run from a 'Wide Ball' shall be scored 'Wide Balls', or if no runs be made one run shall be so scored. The Striker may be out from a 'Wide Ball' if he breaks Laws 38 or 42, and either Batsman may be run out, or given out if he break Laws 36 or 40.

BYE AND LEG BYE

30. If the ball, not having been called 'Wide' or 'No Ball', pass the Striker without touching his bat or person, and any runs be obtained, the Umpire shall call or signal 'Bye'; but if the ball touch any part of the Striker's dress or person except his hand holding the bat, and any run be obtained, the Umpire shall call or signal 'Leg-Bye'; such runs to be scored 'Byes' and 'Leg-Byes' respectively.

NOTES

1. Leg-byes which result from the unintentional deflection of the ball by any part of the striker's person other than the hand holding the bat, whether he has played at the ball or not, are fair. If the umpire is not entirely satisfied that the act was unintentional he shall

call 'Dead Ball' as soon as he sees that the fielding side have no chance of dismissing either batsman as an immediate result of such deflection.

2. The umpire signals 'Bye' by raising an open hand above the head, and 'Leg-Bye' by touching a raised knee with the hand.

THE WICKET IS DOWN

31. The wicket shall be held to be 'Down' if either the ball or the Striker's bat or person completely removes either bail from the top of the stumps, or, if both bails be off, strikes a stump out of the ground. Any player may use his hand or arm to put the wicket down or, even should the bails be previously off, may pull up a stump, provided always that the ball is held iu the hand or hands so used.

NOTES

1. A wicket is not 'down' merely on account of the disturbance of a bail, but it is 'down' if a bail in falling from the wickt lodges between two of the stumps.

2. If one bail is off, it is sufficient for the purpose of this Law to dislodge the remaining one in any of the ways stated, or to strike any of the three stumps out of the ground.

3. If, owing to the strength of the wind, the captains have agreed to dispense with the use of bails (*see* Law 8, Note 2), the decision as to when the wicket is 'down' is one for the umpires to decide on the facts before them. In such circumstances the wicket would be held to be 'down' even though a stump has not been struck out of the ground.

4. If the wicket is broken while the ball is in play, it is not the umpire's duty to remake the wicket until the ball has become 'dead'. A fieldsman, however, may remake the wicket in such circumstances.

5. For the purpose of this and other Laws the term 'person' includes a player's dress as defined in Law 25, Note 4.

OUT OF HIS GROUND

32. A Batsman shall be held to be 'Out of his ground' unless some part of his bat in hand or of his person be grounded behind the line of the Popping Crease.

BATSMAN RETIRING

33. A Batsman may retire at any time, but may not resume his innings without the consent of the opposing Captain, and then only on the fall of a wicket.

NOTE

1. When a batsman has retired owing to illness, injury, or some other unavoidable cause, his innings is recorded as 'Retired, Not out,' but otherwise as a completed innings to be recorded as 'Retired, Out.'

BOWLED

34. The Striker is out 'Bowled' – If the wicket be bowled down, even if the ball first touch his bat or person.

NOTE

1. The striker, after playing the ball, is out 'Bowled' if he then kicks or hits it on to his wicket before the completion of his stroke.

2. The striker is out 'Bowled' under this Law when

the ball is deflected on to his wicket off his person, even though a decision against him might be justified under Law 39 L.B.W.

CAUGHT

35. The Striker is out 'Caught' – If the ball, from a stroke of the bat or of the hand holding the bat, but not the wrist, be held by a Fieldsman before it touch the ground, although it be hugged to the body of the catcher, or be accidentally lodged in his dress. The Fieldsman must have both is feet entirely within the playing area at the instant the catch is completed.

NOTES

1. Provided the ball does not touch the ground, the hand holding it may do so in effecting a catch.

2. The umpire is justified in disregarding the fact that the ball has touched the ground, or has been carried over the boundary provided that a catch has in fact been completed prior to such occurrence.

3. The fact that a ball has touched the striker's person before or after touching his bat does not invalidate a catch.

4. The striker may be 'Caught' even if the fieldsman has not touched the ball with his hands, including the case of a ball lodging in the wicket-keeper's pads.

5. A fieldsman standing within the playing area may lean against the boundary to catch the ball, and this may be done even if the ball has passed over the boundary.

6. If the striker lawfully plays the ball a second time he may be out under this Law, but only if the ball has

H

not touched the ground since being first struck.

7. The striker may be caught off any obstruction within the playing area provided it has not previously been decided on as a boundary.

HANDLED THE BALL

36. Either Batsman is out 'Handled the Ball' – If he touch it while in play with his hands, unless it be done at the request of the opposite side.

NOTES

1. A hand holding the bat is regarded as part of it for the purposes of Laws 36, 37, and 39.

2. The correct entry in the score book when a batsman is given out under this Law is 'Handled the Ball,' and the bowler does not get credit for the wicket.

HIT THE BALL TWICE

37. The Striker is out 'Hit the ball twice' – If the ball be struck or be stopped by any part of his person, and he wilfully strike it again, except for the sole purpose of guarding his wicket, which he may do with his bat or any part of his person, other than his hands. No runs except those which result from an overthrow shall be scored from a ball lawfully struck twice.

NOTES

1. It is for the umpire to decide whether the ball has been so struck a second time legitimately or not. The umpire may regard the fact that a run is attempted as evidence of the batsmen's intention to take advantage

of the second stroke, but it is not conclusive.

2. A batsman may not attempt to hit the ball twice, if in so doing he baulks the wicket-keeper or any fieldsman attempting to make a catch.

3. This Law is infringed if the striker, after playing the ball and without any request from the opposite side, uses his bat to return the ball to a fieldsman.

4. The correct entry in the score book when the striker is given out under this Law is 'Hit the ball twice,' and the bowler does not get credit for the wicket.

HIT WICKET

38. The Striker is out 'Hit wicket' – If in playing at the ball he hit down his wicket with his bat or any part of his person.

NOTES

1. The Striker is 'Out' under this Law if:

(i) In making a second stroke to keep the ball out of his wicket he hits it down.

(ii) While playing at the ball, but not otherwise, his wicket is broken by his cap or hat falling, or by part of his bat.

2. A batsman is not out for breaking the wicket with his bat or person while in the act of running.

L.B.W.

39. The Striker is out 'Leg before wicket' – If with any part of his person except his hand, which is in a straight line between wicket and wicket, even though the point of impact be above the level of the bails, he intercept a ball which has not first touched his bat or hand, and which, in

the opinion of the Umpire, shall have, or would have, pitched on a straight line from the Bowler's wicket to the Striker's wicket, or shall have pitched on the off-side of the Striker's wicket, provided always that the ball would have hit the wicket.

NOTE

1. The word 'hand' used in this Law should be interpreted as the hand holding the bat.

2. A batsman is only 'Out' under this Law if *all* the four following questions are answered in the affirmative.

  (i) Would the ball have hit the wicket?

  (ii) Did the ball pitch on a straight line between wicket and wicket (and this cause includes a ball intercepted full pitch by the striker), or did it pitch on the offside of the striker's wicket?

  (iii) Was it part of the striker's person other than the hand which first intercepted the ball?

  (iv) Was that part of the striker's person in a straight line between wicket and wicket at the moment of impact, irrespective of the height of the point of impact?

OBSTRUCTING THE FIELD

40. Either Batsman is out 'Obstructing the field' – If he wilfully obstruct the opposite side; should such wilful obstruction by either Batsmen prevent a ball from being caught it is the Striker who is out.

NOTES

1. The umpire must decide whether the obstruction was 'wilful' or not. The involuntary interception by a

batsman while running of a throw in is not in itself an offence.

2. The correct entry in the score book when a batsman is given out under this Law is 'Obstructing the field,' and the bowler does not get credit for the wicket.

RUN OUT

41. Either Batsman is out 'Run out' – If in running or at any time, while the ball is in play, he be out of his ground, and his wicket be put down by the opposite side. If the batsmen have crossed each other, he that runs for the wicket which is put down is out; if they have not crossed, he that has left the wicket which is put down is out. But unless he attempt to run, the Striker shall not be given 'Run out' in the circumstances stated in Law 42, even should 'No Ball' have been called.

NOTE

1. If the ball is played on to the opposite wicket, neither batsman is liable to be 'Run out' unless the ball has been touched by a fieldsman before the wicket is put down.

STUMPED

42. A striker is out 'Stumped' – If in receiving a ball, not being a 'No Ball,' delivered by the Bowler, he be out of his ground otherwise than in attempting a run, and the wicket be put down by the Wicket-keeper without the intervention of another fieldsman. Only when the ball has touched the bat or person of the Striker may the Wicket-keeper take it in front of the wicket for this purpose.

NOTE

1. The striker may be 'Stumped' if the wicket is broken by a ball rebounding from the wicket-keeper's person.

THE WICKET-KEEPER

43. The Wicket-keeper shall remain wholly behind the wicket until a ball delivered by the Bowler touches the bat or person of the Striker, or passes the wicket, or until the Striker attempts a run. Should the Wicket-keeper contravene this Law, the Striker shall not be out except under Laws 36, 37, 40, and 41 and then only subject to Law 46.

NOTE

1. This Law is provided to secure to the striker his right to play the ball and to guard his wicket without interference from the wicket-keeper. The striker may not be penalised if in the legitimate defence of his wicket he interferes with the wicket-keeper, except as provided for in Law 37, Note 2.

THE FIELDSMAN

44. The Fieldsman may stop the ball with any part of his person, but if he wilfully stop it otherwise five runs shall be added to the run or runs already made; if no run has been made five shall be scored. The penalty shall be added to the score of the Striker if the ball has been struck, but otherwise to the score of Byes, Leg Byes, No Balls or Wides as the case may be.

NOTES

1. A fieldsman must not use his cap, etc., for the purpose of fielding a ball.

2. The five runs are a penalty and the batsmen do not change ends.

(E) – DUTIES OF THE UMPIRES

45. Before the toss for innings, the Umpires shall acquaint themselves with any special regulations, and shall agree with both Captains on any other conditions affecting the conduct of the match; shall satisfy themselves that the wickets are properly pitched; and shall agree, between themselves on the watch or clock to be followed during play.

NOTES

1. Apart from 'Special Regulations' (*see* Law 10, Note 1), other conditions of play within the framework of the Laws are frequently necessary, *e.g.* Hours of play, Intervals, etc.

2. The captains are entitled to know which clock or watch will be followed during play.

46. Before and during a match the Umpires shall ensure that the conduct of the game and the implements are used strictly in accordance with the Laws; they are the sole judges of fair and unfair play, and the final judges of the fitness of the ground, the weather and the light for play in the event of the decision being left to them; all disputes shall be determined by them, and if they disagree the actual state of things shall continue. The Umpires shall change ends after each side has had one innings.

NOTES

1. An umpire should stand where he can best see any act upon which his decision may be required. Subject to this overriding consideration the umpire at the bowler's end should stand where he does not interfere with either the bowler's run up or the striker's view. If the other umpire wishes to stand on the off instead of the leg side of the pitch, he should obtain the permission of the captain of the fielding side and inform the batsman.

2. The umpires must not allow the attitude of the players or spectators to influence their decisions under the Laws.

3. A code of signals for umpires is laid down in the Notes to the relevant Laws; but an umpire must call as well as signal, if necessary, to inform the players and scorers.

4. FAIR AND UNFAIR PLAY. (i) The umpires are entitled to intervene without appeal in the case of unfair play, but should not otherwise interfere with the progress of the game, except as required to do so by the Laws.

(ii) In the event of a player failing to comply with the instructions of an umpire or criticising his decisions, the umpires should in the first place request the captains to take action, and if this proves ineffective, report the incident forthwith to the executives of the teams taking part in the match.

(iii) It is illegal for a player to lift the seam of the ball in order to obtain a better hold. In such a case the umpire will if necessary change the ball for one which has had similar wear, and will warn the captain that the practice is unfair. The use of resin, wax, etc., by bowlers is also unfair, but a bowler may dry the ball when wet on a towel or with sawdust.

(iv) An umpire is justified in intervening under this Law should any player of the fielding side incommode the striker by any noise or motion while he is receiving a ball.

(v) It is the duty of umpires to intervene and prevent players from causing damage to the pitch which may assist the bowlers.

(vi) The persistent bowling of fast short-pitched balls at the batsman is unfair if, in the opinion of the umpire at the bowler's end, it constitutes a systematic attempt at intimidation. In such event he must adopt the following procedure:

(*a*) When he decides that such bowling is becoming persistent he forthwith 'cautions' the bowler.

(*b*) If this 'caution' is ineffective, he informs the captain of the fielding side and the other umpire of what has occurred.

(*c*) Should the above prove ineffective, the umpire at the bowler's end must:

  (i) At the first repetition call 'Dead Ball,' when the over is regarded as completed.

  (ii) Direct the captain of the fielding side to take the bowler off forthwith. The captain shall take the bowler off as directed.

  (iii) Report the occurrence to the captain of the batting side as soon as an interval of play takes place.

A bowler who has been 'taken off' as above may not bowl again during the same innings.

(vii) Any attempt by the batsmen to *steal a run* during the bowler's run up is unfair. Unless the bowler throws the ball at either wicket (*see* Laws 26, Note 3, and 27, Note 2), the umpire should call 'Dead Ball' as soon as the batsmen cross in any such attempt to run, after which they return to their original wickets.

(viii) No player shall leave the field for the purpose of having a rub down or shower while play is actually in progress.

5. GROUND, WEATHER AND LIGHT. (i) Unless agreement to the contrary is made before the start of a match, the captains (during actual play the batsmen at the wickets may deputise for their captain (may elect to decide in regard to the fitness of the ground, weather or light for play; otherwise or in the event of disagreement, the Umpires are required to decide.

(ii) Play should only be suspended when the conditions are so bad that it is unreasonable or dangerous for it to continue. The ground is unfit for play when water stands on the surface or when it is so wet or slippery as to deprive the batsmen or bowlers of a reasonable foothold, or the fieldsman of the power of free movement. Play should *not* be suspended merely because the grass is wet and the ball slippery.

(iii) After any suspension of play, the captains, or, if the decision has been left to them, the Umpires, unaccompanied by any of the players, will without further instructions carry out an inspection immediately the conditions improve, and will continue to inspect at intervals. Immediately the responsible parties decide that play is possible, they must call upon the players to resume the game.

APPEALS

47. The Umpires shall not order a Batsman out unless appealed to by the other side which shall be done prior to the delivery of the next ball, and before 'Time' is called under Law 18. The Umpire at the Bowler's wicket shall answer appeals before the other Umpire in all cases except those arising out of Laws 38 or 42 and out of Law 41 for run out at the Striker's wicket. In any case in which an Umpire is unable to give a decision, he shall appeal to the other Umpire whose decision shall be final.

NOTES

1. An appeal, 'How's that?' covers all ways of being out (within the jurisdiction of the umpire appealed to), unless a specific way of getting out is stated by the person asking. When either umpire has given a batsman 'Not out' the other umpire may answer any appeal within his jurisdiction, provided it is made in time.

2. The umpire signals 'Out' by raising the index finger above the head. If the batsman is not out, the umpire calls 'Not out'.

3. An umpire may alter his decision provided that such alteration is made promptly.

4. Nothing in this Law prevents an umpire before giving a decision from consulting the other umpire on a point of fact which the latter may have been in a better position to observe. An umpire should not appeal to the other umpire in cases on which he could give a decision, merely because he is unwilling to give that

decision. If after consultation he is still in any doubt, the principle laid down in Law 46 applies and the decision will be in favour of the batsman.

5. The umpires should intervene if satisfied that a batsman, not having been given out, has left his wicket under a misapprehension.

6. Under Law 25 the ball is 'Dead' on 'Over' being called; this does not invalidate an appeal made prior to the first ball of the following 'Over', provided the bails have not been removed by both umpires after 'Time' has been called.

NOTES FOR SCORERS AND UMPIRES

1. (a) Law 4 explains the status of the scorers in relation to the umpires.

(b) During the progress of the game, if two scorers have been appointed, they should frequently check the total to ensure that the score sheets agree.

(c) The following method of entering 'No Balls' and 'Wides' (Laws 27 and 29) in the score sheet is recommended:

   (i) If no run is scored from the bat off a 'No Ball', the latter should be entered as an 'Extra', and and dot placed in the bowling analysis with a circle round it to show that the ball does not count in the over.

   (ii) If runs are scored from the bat off a 'No Ball', they should be credited to the striker, and entered in the bowling analysis with a circle round the figure. Such runs count against the bowler in his analysis even though the ball does not count in the over.

(iii) All runs scored from 'Wide Balls' are entered as 'Extras', and inserted in the bowler's analysis with a cross to indicate that the ball does not count in the over.

2. The following code of signalling between the umpires and the scorers has been approved:

Boundaries – by waving the hand from side to side.

A boundary six – by raising both arms above the head.

Byes – by raising the open hand above the head.

Leg Byes – by touching a raised knee with the hand.

Wides – by extending both arms horizontally.

No Balls – by extending one arm horizontally.

The decision 'Out,' – by raising the index finger above the head.

'One Short' – by bending the arm upwards and by touching the top of the nearest shoulder with the tips of the fingers of one hand.

3. If the above instructions are properly carried out, cases of disagreement as regards the scores and the results of matches should not occur.

It is, however, important that the captains should satisfy themselves of the correctness of the scores on the conclusion of play, as errors cannot subsequently be corrected.

It should be noted that, in general, by accepting the result notified by the scorers, the captain of the losing side has thereby acquiesced in the 'playing out or giving up' of the match as stated in Law 22.

REGULATIONS FOR DRYING THE PITCH AND GROUND IN FIRST-CLASS MATCHES IN THE UNITED KINGDOM

N.B. – *These regulations are primarily designed for First-class Cricket, and their application in whole or in part is at the discretion of the ground, etc., authorities.*

1. Except as provided below, the existing regulations in regard to the rolling of the pitch and the fitness of the ground for play shall apply. (*See* Laws 10, 12 and 46).

2. (i) To enable play to proceed with the least possible delay after rain, the groundsman shall adopt every practical means to protect or rid the surface of the ground, *other than the pitch*, of water or dampness at any time except while play is in progress.

(ii) Prior to tossing for choice of innings the artificial drying of the pitch and outfield shall be at the discretion of the Groundsman. Thereafter and throughout the match the drying of the outfield may be undertaken at any time by the Groundsman, but the drying of the pitch shall be carried out only on the instructions and under the supervision of the Umpires. The Umpires shall be empowered to have the pitch dried without a reference to the Captains at any time they are of the opinion that it is unfit for play.

(iii) In wet weather, the umpires shall see that the foot-holes made by the bowlers and batsmen are cleaned, dried and filled up with sawdust at any time during the match, although the game is not actually in progress.

The groundsman, without instructions from the umpires, may also clean out in this way foot-holes, provided they are not on any part of the pitch, more than 3 ft. 6 ins. in front of the Popping creases.

The drying of the footholds on the pitch itself may be undertaken, as directed by the Umpires, at any time. The umpires may also direct the Groundsman to protect against further rain marks made by the bowlers, even though they be more than 3 ft. 6 ins. in front of the popping creases, provided they are not between wicket and wicket, with loose sawdust, which, however, shall be removed prior to the resumption of play.

(iv) The umpires shall ascertain from the groundsman before the commencement of a match, what equipment is available for drying the pitch artificially.

Any roller may be used, if the umpires think desirable but only (except as laid down in paragraph (2) (v)) for the purpose of drying the pitch and making it fit for play, and not otherwise. This would allow umpires to roll the pitch after drying it, say with a light roller, for a minute or two, should they consider it desirable.

(v) When the artificial drying of the pitch, under the supervision of the umpires, coincides with any interval during the match, after the toss for choice of innings, the umpires, and not the captain of the batting side, shall select the roller to be used.

(vi) The fact that the umpires may have dried the pitch artificially does not take the decision as regards the fitness of the pitch and ground for play out of the hands of the captains, even though the umpires may have selected the roller to be used for the drying process. Law 46, Note 5 (i) is applicable in such cases.

INDEX TO THE LAWS OF CRICKET